UNDERGRADUATE RESEARCH IN DANCE

Undergraduate Research in Dance: A Guide for Students supplies tools for scaffolding research skills alongside examples of undergraduate research in dance scholarship. Dance can be studied as an expressive embodied art form with physical, cognitive, and affective domains, and as an integral part of society, history, and vast areas of interdisciplinary content. To this end, the guidance provided by this book will equip future dance professionals with the means to move the field of dance forward.

Chapters 1–9 guide students through the fundamentals of research methods, providing a foundation to help students get started in understanding research protocols and processes. Students will learn skills such as how to choose a research topic, refine research questions, conduct literature reviews, cite sources, synthesize and analyze data, develop conclusions and results, and present their findings. Chapters 10–19 detail forms of undergraduate research in a rich diversity of fields within dance that are taught in many collegiate dance programs including dance therapy, history, science, psychology, education, and technology, in addition to public scholarship, choreography, and interdisciplinary topics. The book also includes a final chapter which provides annotated online resources, and many of its chapters are supported by examples of abstracts of capstone projects, senior theses, and conference presentations by undergraduate researchers across the United States.

Suitable for both professors and students, *Undergraduate Research in Dance* is an ideal reference book for any course that has a significant opportunity for the creation of new knowledge, or as an essential interdisciplinary connection between dance and other disciplines.

Lynnette Young Overby is Professor of Theatre and Dance at the University of Delaware and serves as Director of Research for Dance and the Child International. She has organized poster sessions for the National Dance Education Organization for several years.

Jenny Olin Shanahan is Assistant Provost for High Impact Practices at Bridgewater State University and has held numerous leadership roles with the Council for Undergraduate Research.

Gregory Young is Professor of Music at Montana State University and has held ongoing posts in conferences of undergraduate research and in curriculum development.

Routledge Undergraduate Research Series

Series Editors: Gregory Young, Montana State University, and Jenny Olin Shanahan, Bridgewater State University

Undergraduate Research in Music
A Guide for Students
Gregory Young and Jenny Olin Shanahan

Undergraduate Research in Art
A Guide for Students
Vaughan Judge, Jenny Olin Shanahan, and Gregory Young

Undergraduate Research in Dance
A Guide for Students
Lynnette Young Overby, Jenny Olin Shanahan, and Gregory Young

https://www.routledge.com/Routledge-Undergraduate-Research-Series/book-series/RURS

UNDERGRADUATE RESEARCH IN DANCE

A Guide for Students

Lynnette Young Overby, Jenny Olin Shanahan, and Gregory Young

Routledge
Taylor & Francis Group

LONDON AND NEW YORK

First published 2019
by Routledge
2 Park Square, Milton Park, Abingdon, Oxon OX14 4RN

and by Routledge
52 Vanderbilt Avenue, New York, NY 10017

Routledge is an imprint of the Taylor & Francis Group, an informa business

British Library Cataloguing in Publication Data
A catalogue record for this book is available from the British Library

Library of Congress Cataloging-in-Publication Data
A catalog record has been requested for this book

ISBN: 978-1-138-48411-5 (hbk)
ISBN: 978-1-138-48412-2 (pbk)
ISBN: 978-1-351-05298-6 (ebk)

Typeset in Bembo
by Taylor & Francis Books

I dedicate this book to my family who have always supported me through writing, choreographing, and continuing to have a much too busy schedule. I deeply appreciate my mother who turned 100 in 2018, and who still takes her line-dance class twice a week; my husband and children, Cordell, Collin, and Casey, and my son-in-law Rodney; and my new grandson Myles Taylor, with whom I am looking forward to many dreams and dances in the future. Lynnette Young Overby.

CONTENTS

ILLUSTRATIONS

Figures

Tables

Box

SERIES FOREWORD

The Routledge Undergraduate Research Series was created to guide students and faculty, particularly in the arts and humanities, working on a wide variety of research and creative projects. After a brief overview, chapters on the research process common to all disciplines follow, and then several chapters that pertain specifically to the discipline. The National Conferences on Undergraduate Research have expanded annually since 1987 to about 4,000 participants. The British Conference on Undergraduate Research has been an annual event since 2011, and the World Congress on Undergraduate Research started in 2016, demonstrating the relevancy of this movement in our changing higher education curriculum.

Gregory Young and Jenny Olin Shanahan
Series Editors

FOREWORD

For centuries, research and development have been the backbone of innovation, progress, and the setting of industry standards in America. Dance—as an art form, education discipline, and industry—is part of this heritage and is critical to the future of America's culture.

Undergraduate research is one of the most important content areas professors can teach in education today. It is critically important dancers destined to the arts, education, or business understand what we have learned from research in the past century; and, equally important, seek to contribute to the knowledge-base for the next century and generations to come. Individually, each of us can make a difference.

The publication *Undergraduate Research in Dance: A Guide for Students* has several different and crucial applications in undergraduate studies. First, it a great resource for any dance faculty member seeking to push the boundaries and energize undergraduate students through a vision—helping them to see unrealized personal and professional potential and growth in research and development. Research is wonderfully engaging, invigorating, and essential to learning and teaching regardless of the genre or environment in which one engages.

Second, wisely, the book should be required reading in dance major, minor, or certification programs so that students become more dance literate in a field having to justify itself in arts and education policy, legislation, and funding. By understanding research before, especially using the *Dance Education Literature and Research descriptive index* (DELRdi) as a resource (https://www.ndeo.org/delrdi), professors and students will know the patterns, trends, and gaps in our knowledge-base and be able to add to that content of knowledge for themselves and future generations.

Third, the book is an ideal resource for all faculty who have included research components into any dance curriculum taught. Not only does the book cover a vast array of dance-centric topics engaging students in both dance arts and education—from performance and choreography to history, therapy, psychology, theory, and science and technology, but also the book instructs in the research process. It guides the undergraduate dance student through research process and product, including how to choose a research topic, refine research questions, carry out literature reviews, cite sources, synthesize and analyze data, develop conclusions and results, write abstracts, and use online resources. Unquestionably, there is a huge need for this well designed and conceptualized resource in undergraduate education.

As the Founding Executive Director of the National Dance Education Organization (NDEO), I am ever grateful to the authors (Lynnette Young Overby, Jenny Shanahan, and Gregory Young) for writing this important book for faculty to use in undergraduate education. NDEO believes so strongly in research in undergraduate education, that we have established an award called the Thomas K, Hagood DELRdi Award of Excellence in Undergraduate Research. We challenge you to become an awardee!

Keep dancing; but, above all, pursue research for yourself and generations to come!

Jane Bonbright, EdD
Founding Executive Director of the NDEO
Director, Online Professional Development Institute/NDEO

PREFACE

Our goals

We wrote this book to help faculty and students in the arts become more accustomed to viewing what they do through the lens of "undergraduate research" (UR), when scholarship and creative activity are included. Participating in URSCA in the dance curriculum is key to accessing its profound benefits, including increased retention and graduation rates, cognitive and emotional development, acquisition of highly valued skills, and preparation for post-baccalaureate opportunities.

Format

The book is divided into two sections. Chapters 1–9 cover some of the fundamentals of research methods, many of which are common to most disciplines. They provide a foundation to help students get started in understanding research protocols and processes. Chapters 10–18 cover UR in dance fields that are taught in many collegiate dance programs. Chapter 19 provides annotated online resources, but certainly not an exhaustive list. Each chapter begins with an inspirational quote, a chapter summary, and then an explanation of the substance of the chapter with examples and ideas for students to pursue. Many of the chapters have examples of abstracts submitted to conferences by undergraduate researchers across the United States.

Students—How to use this text

A brief glance at the table of contents reveals that this text does not necessarily have to be read in order from the first chapter to the last, but rather it is intended as a guide to be consulted throughout the different facets of student research projects. There is no one perfect way to progress through a UR experience in dance, especially because there are so many different areas to explore. Dance science, for example, may be quite a different experience than a research study in Dance education. So with the guidance of the instructor, use the tools in the first half of the book as needed for your research/creativity, and read about a wide variety of student examples in the areas that interest you in the second half of the book. Be sure to glance through the online resources and delve more deeply into those sites and files that interest you. It might also be helpful to create your own set of online resources and have it handy for future reference.

Conclusion

This text can be used by dance majors from their first semester until they begin a capstone course as a tool to build awareness about the broad field of dance. In capstone courses it can serve not only as the course textbook, but also as a more specific guide for the whole process of choosing a topic and seeing it through to completion. Completing successful UR projects in dance and disseminating the results at conferences and in publications will promote this activity and serve as a model for other dance students in the future.

ACKNOWLEDGMENTS

This book would not be possible without the contributions of former and current University of Delaware students and dance professionals who made major contributions to this book.

Special thanks to Teresa Heiland for her contributions of online dance notation resources; Sharon Goodill for sharing her expertise in the development of the Dance Therapy chapter; Rachel M. DeLauder—Senior Dance Minor at the University of Delaware who has found her voice through her passion for Dance Science and used that passion to author the dance science chapter; Mary Lynn Babcock who provided a view into course content and research possibilities in the Dance Technology chapter; Lucy Font and Megan Lamotte, former ArtsBridge scholars and authors, who contributed to the Dance Education chapter. A. T. Moffett, collaborator on several arts-based research projects, for providing background information and guidelines for the implementation and assessment in the Arts-Based Research chapter; April Singleton, Sophomore University of Delaware student who gathered information and organized the Online Resources chapter.

I also want to acknowledge the contributions of Harriet Tsugranes for locating, editing, and organizing dance minor capstone projects, and students who shared their reflections as ArtsBridge scholars, dance capstone students and scholar/artists including: Benjamin Dutton, Alexis Trench, Michael Rowley, Nick Sisofo, Amanda Boccardi, Rachel Austin, Allison Blackwell, Ikira Peace, Dominique Oppenheimer, Rebecca Hurlock, Heather Levine, Melissa Brower, Andrea Bianculli, and Emily Ferestein. Thank you, Ann-Marie Sylvia, a graduate student at Bridgewater State University for creating the index.

CONTRIBUTORS

Authors

Lynnette Young Overby is a Professor of Theatre and Dance at the University of Delaware, and Deputy Director of the Community Engagement Initiative. She is the author of over 40 publications including 12 edited or authored books. Public Scholarship in Dance was published in the fall of 2015; Dance: Current Selected Research Volume 9 was published in 2018 with co-editor Billie Lepczyk. Dr. Overby also has a record of over 100 major presentations and performances, and is the recipient of the 2018 National Dance Education Lifetime Achievement Award.

Jenny Olin Shanahan is Assistant Provost for High-Impact Practices at Bridgewater State University in Massachusetts, where she supports undergraduate research and other transformative learning programs. She holds a PhD in English from Marquette University and has taught research, literature, and writing for over 20 years. Dr. Shanahan is co-author of Undergraduate Research in Music (Routledge) and over a dozen articles and chapters on undergraduate research. Her research focuses on inclusion and equity in high-impact practices, excellence in mentoring students in scholarly work, and scaffolding research across the curriculum.

Gregory Young has served as Assistant Dean of the College of Arts & Architecture, director of the School of Music, Vice Provost for Undergraduate Education and founding director of the Undergraduate Scholars Program at Montana State University. Dr. Young has published several articles with undergraduates as co-authors, and has given invited talks in Italy, Spain, and the United States on correlations between Music and Architecture. Other interdisciplinary undergraduate research classes have included Music and the Brain, and Music and Economics. He is a former treasurer and chair of the National Conference on Undergraduate Research, and a councilor in the Arts & Humanities division of the Council on Undergraduate Research (CUR). He has done many custom workshops on undergraduate research and facilitated at CUR Institutes.

Dance professionals

Authors

Mary Lynn Babcock
Affiliation: University of North Texas.
Publication history includes published journal articles, book chapters and essays in Research in Dance Education, Journal of Modern Education Review, Global Movements: Dance, Place, and Hybridity (O. Kuhlke and A. Pine, Eds.), and Dance: Current Selected Research Volume 9 (L. Overby and B. Lepczyk, Eds.)

Sharon W. Goodill
Affiliation: Drexel University.
Dr. Goodill has authored or co-authored over 35 publications, which include both peer-reviewed and invited journal articles, book chapters, a white paper for the American Dance Therapy Association, and one single-author book. Journals in which her work has appeared include the American Journal of Dance Therapy, The Journal of Arts in Psychotherapy, the Journal of Allied Health, and the Journal of Alternative Therapies in Health and Medicine.

Ann-Thomas Moffett
Affiliation: Washington College.
Ann-Thomas has published articles in The Journal of Dance Education, and Research in Dance Education.

University of Delaware Students and Alumni

Authors

Rachel M. DeLauder
Senior, University of Delaware; expected graduation 2019.

Lucy Font
University of Delaware; graduate 2016.
Publication history includes an Honors Thesis, University of Delaware, titled "Adding Movement to Subtract Monotony: The Effects of a Dance Integrated Mathematics Curriculum on the Engagement of Students from Low-Income Homes".

Megan LaMotte
University of Delaware; graduate 2015. Publication history includes The Journal of Dance Education.

April Singleton
Sophomore, University of Delaware; expected graduation 2021.

1

OVERVIEW

Lynnette Young Overby and Gregory Young

Dance is the hidden language of the soul of the body.

(Graham, n.d.)

Summary

This chapter outlines the undergraduate research (UR) environment and where dance fits into it, focusing on the benefits of reframing some of the excellent creative work already being done in colleges and universities. Within that context ideas are shared as to the importance of UR, desired learning outcomes, how knowledge and art are created, and how to get the most out of this book. Students from freshman through senior year will begin to understand how their learning can be linked to the discovery of knowledge, while they become more engaged in the process. This interactive pedagogy is much more interesting than traditional classroom lecture-style learning, and the use of the term "research" is certainly not limited to the sciences and/or related fields.

Introduction

Over the last 40 years in the United States, UR activity in colleges and universities has been increasing dramatically, led initially by science professors needing help in laboratories. Thanks to national organizations such as the Council on Undergraduate Research (CUR) and the National Conference on Undergraduate Research (NCUR), these activities have been spreading rapidly into all disciplines. In fact, even though CUR was started by chemists at primarily undergraduate institutions in 1978 as a way of collaborating with undergraduates in their research labs, the biggest division of CUR at the present time is arts and humanities.

NCUR began in 1987 as a celebration of UR in all disciplines open to all colleges and universities, and currently registers about 3,500 student presenters and 500 faculty mentors annually. In 2011 the first British Conference on Undergraduate Research (BCUR) was held, and it continues annually with the recent addition of Posters in Parliament, modeled after Posters on the Hill in the United States. The first Australian Conference on Undergraduate Research (ACUR) was held in 2012, and it too has Posters in Parliament now. The first World Congress for Undergraduate Researchers (WorldCUR) was held in Qatar in November 2016 (Council on Undergraduate Research, 2016).

UR is a high-impact practice that benefits students across demographic groups and disciplines, especially underrepresented minority students. Yet many UR opportunities are highly selective and still predominantly in the lab sciences; much less so in disciplines such as dance, where creative activity abounds but research and scholarship have not been the main focus, at least with undergraduates. URSCA refers to "undergraduate research, scholarship and creative activities," and is seen by many as being more inclusive. Faculty and students in the arts are becoming more accustomed to viewing what they do through the lens of UR. Participating in URSCA in the dance curriculum is key to accessing its profound benefits, including increased retention and graduation rates, cognitive and emotional development, acquisition of highly valued skills, and preparation for post-baccalaureate opportunities.

Undergraduates who engage in research and creative scholarship demonstrate significant gains in the very learning outcomes most highly valued not only by their professors, but also by their future employers: creative and critical thinking, problem-solving and analysis, intellectual curiosity, adaptability, and oral and written communication. Participation in the high-impact practice of UR transforms students, during their college careers—with deeper engagement and marked academic gains—and well into their post-baccalaureate careers.

Where dance fits into the UR movement

As learning in college becomes more active, and students desire greater input into their own education, UR and creative activities become more significant and more interesting. Since search engines such as Google can help students find a plethora of content, and YouTube provides a great array of dance and instruction at our fingertips, learning how to actually create knowledge, how to tap into our creativity, and how to advance the discipline of dance, should take center stage, so to speak.

There are many different terms for UR, including "inquiry," "scholarship," "creative activity," and "creative scholarship." These terms are used interchangeably; although scholars in various disciplines often have preferences for the ways they describe their work. Many people involved in CUR, especially in its arts and humanities division, use URSCA. Whether you prefer one term over another, or your university has a program that uses certain terms, the term itself does not matter as much as what is it indicates: scholarly work that is faculty-mentored, original, disciplinarily appropriate, and disseminated (Osborn & Karukstis, 2009). We generally avoid some of the science terms such as "hypothesis," and "methodology" when writing about original choreography, for example, and could substitute the terms such as "background research," and "choreographic forms." Students in dance or any other field also benefit from the cross-pollination that occurs when considering how UR is practiced in disciplines that are quite different from their own, and when they explore the different terminology.

How can students do something original when professors, scholars, composers, theorists, and other dance practitioners have already done so much research? One way is to take an interdisciplinary approach, viewing dance from the perspective of another discipline. For example, there has been little research published on the correlations between dance and economics. Dance and the brain offers topics that are ripe for discovery, especially with new advances in medical technology that allow even undergraduates the opportunity to view brain wave activity while students are dancing or watching dance. Several chapters in this book provide examples of interdisciplinary projects.

Students do not have to follow an interdisciplinary path because there are many standard activities in undergraduate dance programs that students and professors have been engaged in for decades that have not generally been regarded as UR. For example, every semester or year, dance concerts that take place where student, faculty, and guest choreographers share their work. Opportunities exist for explorations of dance history, science, psychology—the list of possible topics is extensive. Some suggestions are indicated in each of the chapters. Since universities and colleges are now stressing the importance of UR campus wide, and students in most disciplines are doing it as a regular part of their education and presenting their findings publicly, dance students would benefit from joining in. Campus-wide celebrations of UR with oral and poster sessions are becoming common on college campuses, but are still dominated by the sciences. These symposia could be enhanced with greater contributions from the arts, including a variety of dance projects. And directors of such events are often open to the idea of using special venues for dance-related projects and allowing different methods of delivery.

Why UR is important

An undergraduate dance curriculum would not be complete without a substantial exploration into the discovery of knowledge, whether that exploration is focused on any one of a variety of topics, such as: the way new dance is created; the effectiveness of different pedagogies; historical revelations or re-discoveries; or innovative techniques, analyses, or practices. Such a study is often undertaken in the latter part of the curriculum, but ideally one should be exposed to the act of discovery and creation as often as possible throughout the program.

When students are asked about their vision for how they would like to learn, many say they want it to be exciting, applicable, social, and interactive. Doing group projects, working alongside professors, having input instead of passively listening, and helping to chart their own pathways, can all be components of UR in dance.

When employers are asked what skills they want future employees to have, many list teamwork, creativity, problem solving, critical thinking, as well as written and oral communication. All of these can be strengthened by a real academic experience in UR and creative activity.

Can UR benefit the student and the professor?

More and more, universities are emphasizing the integration of scholarship and teaching, linking student learning with the discovery of knowledge, and making active learning a hallmark experience of an undergraduate degree. One of the best ways to accomplish all of these is to have a professor carve out a small piece of his/her own larger research project, and assign it to a student. Examples abound in chemistry, where researchers can be much more productive in the laboratory with the help of undergraduate researchers, and the students learn the complex process of original research in their field. In the arts and humanities, and particularly in dance, professors often view their research/creativity as individual creative pursuits, and published articles and dance projects are usually listed with only one author/choreographer. However, with a little creativity, win-win situations can be created that increase productivity for the professors and that provide first-hand experience on the front lines of the creation of art or original research for the students.

Throughout the chapters there will be examples and abstracts created by undergraduate dance minor students as part of several UR opportunities at the University of Delaware. I (Overby) have personally benefited by having the assistance of students to pursue several research/creative activity projects. From photo-voice projects, where undergraduate students have served as interviewers, to ArtsBridge scholars, where students have conducted quasi-experimental studies to determine the effectiveness of arts integration, to arts-based research projects that provide audiences with insight into a social issue, the benefits have been win-win for me and for the student researcher. Results have included contributions to a book series (*Dance: Current Selected Research*), journal articles in *Journal of Dance Education*, and many national and international presentations, where I share authorship and presentation space with my undergraduate students.

How to use this text

A brief glance at the table of contents reveals that this text does not necessarily have to be read in order from the first chapter to the last, but rather it is intended as a guide to be consulted throughout the different facets of student research projects. There is no one perfect way to progress through an UR experience in dance, especially because there are so many different areas to explore. Choreography, for example, will be quite a different experience than a quantitative research study in dance education. So with the guidance of the instructor, use the tools in the first half of the book as needed for your research/creativity, and read about a wide variety of student examples in the areas that interest you in the second half of the book. Be sure to glance through the online resources and delve more deeply into those sites and files that interest you. It might also be helpful to create your own set of online resources and have it handy for future reference.

Conclusion

This text can be used by dance majors and minors from their first semester until they begin their capstone course as a tool to build awareness about the broad field of dance. In the capstone course it can serve not only as the course textbook, but also as a more specific guide for the whole process of choosing a topic and seeing it through to completion. Completing successful UR projects in dance and disseminating the results at conferences and in publications will promote this activity and serve as a model for other students in the future.

Questions for discussion

1. What is the difference between creativity in science and creativity in dance?
2. How do the terms "inquiry," "creativity," "scholarship," and "research" differ?
3. Why do employers prefer students who have done UR?
4. Do all professors do research, and how much do they need to do?

References

Council on Undergraduate Research. (2016). Council on Undergraduate Research: Learning through research. Retrieved from https://www.cur.org

Graham, M. (n.d.). Martha Graham Quotes. Retrieved from https://www.brainyquote. com/quotes/martha_graham_379056?src=t_dance

Osborn, J. M., & Karukstis, K. K. (2009). The benefits of undergraduate research, scholarship, and creative activity. In M. Boyd, & J. Wesemann (Eds.), *Broadening Participation in Undergraduate Research: Fostering Excellence and Enhancing the Impact* (pp. 41–53). Washington, DC: Council on Undergraduate Research.

2

LITERATURE REVIEWS

Jenny Olin Shanahan

Summary

A literature review is an organized, informed discussion of published works that are significant to the subject of study. It conveys the relationship between the present study and what has already been published in the field. By reviewing the literature, scholars join important conversations in the discipline, with critical understanding of what others have said, how the voices in the conversation relate to one another, and where they might add insight.

Purpose and format of a literature review

Conducting research on dance and reporting on its results is a professional way of joining a vibrant, ongoing conversation about the field. Contributing to that interesting conversation entails understanding what others have said, how the voices in the conversation relate to one another, and where further insight might be added. To contribute meaningfully to the conversation scholars need to study published material (the "literature") related to the topic. Much like other reviews, a literature review is an analysis of that published material.

A literature review provides context for your research study by explaining what is already known and what needs further exploration. In doing so, it establishes your credibility as a researcher, demonstrating that your project or study did not emerge from "out of the blue," but from thoughtful consideration of what has been published already and how your work fits into that framework. The literature review should accomplish three main objectives:

- Briefly summarize the salient points of the most important publications on the topic of study;

- Explain the relationships among those published works (e.g., how a major study changed the field, why some scholars came to differing conclusions on a key question, how the introduction of a new factor or variable in one study led to surprising results);
- Identify gaps in the literature—the questions or issues that have not yet been examined.

That third objective, identifying gaps in the research literature, is critical to showing the need for your study. The literature review shows that you have read and analyzed important sources on the topic, and at least one significant question has not been addressed or has not been definitively answered. That is the gap your study seeks to fill.

Literature review vs. annotated bibliography

The format or structure of a literature review is different from that of an annotated bibliography, which summarizes or describes one source after another in a few sentences each. If your professor assigns an annotated bibliography as well as a literature review for your research, you would complete the annotated bibliography first, as it represents your first pass through the relevant literature. Although annotated bibliographies usually include a brief evaluation of each source, each entry is its own individual item, listed in alphabetical order by author last name. The bibliography entries do not connect with each other except for the fact that they are on the same general topic. A literature review, however, is not in a list. It is a narrative that could stand on its own as a coherent essay, with unified paragraphs and transitions between points. Your literature review allows you to "tell the story" of what scholars already understand about the topic and how they have informed your own study. Specific strategies for organizing your literature review are laid out later in this chapter.

Joining a scholarly conversation

Almost everyone has had the irritating experience of being interrupted from what had been an interesting conversation by someone who does not know what has already been said but jumps in with opinions anyway. Sometimes the interrupter spouts unrelated ideas or rehashes a point from which the conversation has already moved on. The interrupter in such cases shows disrespect to the people who have already been engaged in the conversation as well as a lack of credibility. The group would probably dismiss the interrupter's ideas, even if they are potentially good ones, because they appear to be random and uninformed. For good reason, most of us have been socialized to join an ongoing conversation in a more respectful way: only after listening for a little while and gaining familiarity with the topic. A new person joining a conversation should ask or wait to hear what the group is talking about or allow someone already involved in the conversation to offer a recap.

That metaphor of joining an ongoing conversation is a useful way of thinking about a literature review. A "conversation" about the topic (or closely related to the topic) has been going on in the field, as represented in the published research literature. Reading the literature allows new scholars in the field to listen to what has been said and join the conversation as informed participants. Only by reading closely, or "listening" to, the previous participants' ideas can you contribute something original and interesting to the conversation, such as a new idea that has not been completely covered already or a question about someone else's point that adds an intriguing dimension to the topic. In other words, by conducting a review of the research literature you avoid "interrupting" a conversation with stale opinions or irrelevant questions; instead, you can knowledgably participate in a discussion of an interesting topic with a group of scholars who also deeply care about it.

Finding appropriate sources

Peer-reviewed sources

For most scholarly projects in dance, the literature review will be based on *peer-reviewed sources*. Peer review is a process of quality-control to ensure that articles and books accepted for publication are accurate and based on valid research methods. Academic journals and book publishers typically rely on rigorous peer-review processes before publishing someone's research. To be considered for publication, a researcher submits an article or chapter to an editor, who reaches out to experts specializing in the author's area of study to ask them to review it. Those experts are the researcher's "peers." Most peer reviews are *double-blind*, meaning that the researcher does not know who is reviewing the work, and reviewers do not know who authored it. Whether they are reviewing "blindly" or not, the reviewers are expected to evaluate the quality of the work impartially. They use their own expertise to determine whether the author conducted a valid and reliable research study, whether the findings or conclusions are sound, and to what degree the research makes an important contribution to the field of study. Peer reviewers usually can accept a work "as is" (perhaps with minor edits) or "with revision" (requiring the author to address particular questions or problems in the next draft). Otherwise, if the work does not meet the standards for research in the discipline, the reviewers reject it. Due to a rigorous process of review that determines whether a work is published or not, peer-reviewed journal articles and books are considered the best quality scholarship. On the spectrum of reliable sources of information, one might think of peer-reviewed articles as opposite to "fake news" on social media. Any information simply made up by the author would be rejected by peer reviewers, who demand evidence of careful methods and accurate reporting. The professional reputations of a journal's or publisher's peer reviewers are as much on the line as those of the authors being published.

This book, for example, went through two peer-review processes. This book began, as most do, as a proposal submitted to a publisher. The proposal included an explanation of the need we saw for such a book, a proposed outline of chapters with brief descriptions of what would be included in each, and a sample chapter. The publisher forwarded the proposal to three experts in the field: dance professors at different universities who mentor undergraduate research and have presented at conferences and/or published on the topic of UR in dance—in other words, the reviewers were our peers. The peer reviewers each made recommendations about additional topics for us to include and other sources for us to consult, and they each recommended to the publisher that we proceed with writing the book. Once a full draft (a *manuscript*) was complete, it went through a different round of peer review, through which we received additional revision suggestions that made the final product considerably stronger.

If a professor or editor asks for a literature review of *peer-reviewed sources*, this is why: only high-quality research studies will inform the work. Researchers are unlikely to be led astray by false or unverified information when they stick to peer-reviewed journals and books. That said, it is sometimes acceptable to include non-peer-reviewed sources in a literature review, especially if the sources can be verified as reliable through other means (more about that later in this chapter) and/or if the topic of study has not received much attention yet from academic scholars. Consider for example a literature review on a contemporary choreographer or an emerging genre of dance. Because the peer-review process takes time, academic articles and books are published many months after the manuscripts are first submitted. Experts in the field of dance, however, may be able to publish informative articles in the popular press in a matter of days. An analysis published in *The New Yorker* is not a peer-reviewed scholarly piece, but it is reliable and therefore may be a valuable part of a literature review.

Library databases

The best place to find peer-reviewed, scholarly articles is in online databases to which your college or university library subscribes. Starting with open-source repositories of scholarship such as Google Scholar is fine, but most academic journal articles are still found in subscription-only databases such as Academic Search Premier, JSTOR, EBSCOhost—especially EBSCO's International Bibliography of Theatre and Dance—and, for the purposes of dance research, the Dance Education Literature and Research descriptive index (DELRdi), Dance in Video: Volumes I and II, and the New York Public Library Dance Catalog, among others.

We recommend consulting with a reference librarian to learn about the relevant online databases for your topic area and how to access them. Many college/university library websites offer online tutorials for using databases. If you prefer a tutorial in-person, a reference librarian may be able to walk you through the basic guidelines for the databases to which the library is subscribed. Knowing the specific parameters for searching each database (e.g., which truncation symbols and Boolean operators it recognizes) helps to make searches more efficient and effective.

Truncation symbols allow users to search for multiple, closely related words at one time. Some databases use # as a truncation symbol, while others use ★ (e.g., educa# for educate, education, educator, and educational; or wom★n for woman and women). Boolean operators are conjunctions (e.g., *and, or*) and other connecting words (e.g., *not*) that are used to include or exclude certain terms from a search. For example, a search for information about the Balanchine Method might use Boolean operators in this way: Balanchine AND Method OR Technique (to include both Balanchine Method and Balanchine Technique, two terms for the same performance style). Another option for that search in many databases is "Balanchine Method," indicating that only results with *Balanchine* and *Method* adjacent to one another will be found. A few databases, though, use single quotation marks for that purpose ('Balanchine Method') and still others do not use quotation marks at all to keep terms together! Until the unlikely day when all database builders will agree on a single system, consulting a reference librarian or a written guide to library databases is essential to finding the right information.

In order to identify relevant books and articles, researchers use a variety of search terms. To yield comprehensive results, reference librarians sometimes recommend making a list of alternative terms and subjects related to your topic area and then conducting database searches using all of those terms. When researchers have trouble locating information, the problem is often that they have not hit upon the precise search terms used in the database. For example, someone researching *dance therapy* may find that using the terms *"Dance Movement Therapy"* and *"Dance Movement Psychotherapy"* (the term used in the United Kingdom) will yield additional results.

Experienced scholars know that the bibliographies of sources already found are excellent resources for identifying additional sources. By reading the titles of books or articles (and the names of journals in which they appear) on bibliographies, researchers can find a rich trove of additional texts to read. If the same source is referenced repeatedly, that is a good indication of its importance in the field. Similarly, when scholars find a particularly useful source, they search to discover what else the author has written and whether the journal has published any similar articles.

Analyzing existing research

In addition to being called "literature," the articles located through database searches are often referred to as *existing research* to differentiate those works from the original research you are conducting in your own study. Articles and books are also called *secondary sources* as a way of contrasting them from the *primary sources* that some studies utilize, such as movement notations, recordings of performances, photos of dancers, diaries, letters, notebooks, and compositions. Secondary sources are articles, books, blog posts, etc. that analyze: (a) other texts (reviews, artwork, historical or legal documents, and other primary sources); (b) video-recordings and photos; (c) historical events and eras; (d) statistical or experimental data; or (e) people's lives, words, or actions.

To do the analysis required for a literature review, we recommend printing hard copies of articles and reading them with a pencil in hand, ready to underline sentences, circle key words, and take notes in the margins. When reading digital copies of articles or library copies of books, using a research journal (a spiral notebook is perfect) can substitute well for writing on a hard copy. Using a form of shorthand that at least you can understand later, you can make note of important points, key terms, and questions that arise as you read. That kind of critical reflection is the vital piece missing from inadequate literature reviews. Giving time and consideration to reflect on, and position yourself in, dialogue with the sources yields a much more nuanced and resonant study than the so-called "research sausage" that is created by throwing together a little from this article, a little from that book, etc. and trying to fit it all into the preformed casing of a "literature review."

Reading reflectively

The following suggestions are a guide for reflective reading of articles in preparation for a literature review.

1. Read the Abstract first, then the Conclusion, before starting the body of the article. That strategy allows you to determine the relevance of the article to the study and, if it is indeed relevant, to boost your comprehension of its main ideas. After reading the Abstract and Conclusion, skim the section headings and subheadings, and look at any figures or graphs. Then begin reading with the end in mind. A clearer sense of the relative importance of each paragraph to the overall article becomes evident, allowing you to know which paragraphs can be skimmed and which need focused attention.

2. The "halo effect" is a cognitive bias that, in this situation, can lead a reader to assume that because an author's work is published in a peer-reviewed journal, the author must be "right," even though scholarly work is rarely definitive. As careful researchers read, they keep their mind open to various perspectives on the topic by alternately accepting the author's viewpoint and then raising questions about the research methods, limitations of the study, strength of the evidence, and the conclusions that are drawn. By following that model and raising questions and identifying the limitations as you read, you will help yourself in two ways: you will be able to draw more interesting and nuanced connections between sources in the literature review when you notice how each argument is constructed, and your analysis could lead to discovery of a "gap" in the research.

3. Approach reading as a multiple-draft process, not unlike the writing process. Scholars re-read some parts of each article, deepening their understanding with each return to the text. Academic writing, in particular, is densely constructed and written for experts in the field. It demands more than a single-shot reading to grasp its meaning and implications. Anyone new to reading and analyzing research literature is likely to feel lost in the complex

sentence structures and specialized terminology. It is written that way not to confuse readers, but to convey as efficiently as possible very sophisticated ideas to a highly educated audience. A metaphor we use with our students is that of a tightly packed suitcase: it took a great deal of planning and care for the author to use the space efficiently; as you "unpack" it you may need to move slowly, examining one item or point at a time, noting its significance before moving to the next.

4. Continually ask how each article or book chapter relates, specifically, to the topic area being explored. Could it help to contextualize the problem? Does it show that your research question remains unanswered? Does it demonstrate how other scholars have attempted to address the question differently than your study will? In this way you can begin painless drafting of other parts of the research paper; for example, an article that corroborates the identified problem can be referenced in the Introduction.

5. Learn the context for each source. Where does it appear (if an article)? What other kinds of articles does that journal publish? When was it written? Have there been more recent and/or more important publications on the matter? (The importance of an article can be determined in part by noting how often it is cited in other articles.) If it is an article that appears on a website or in a periodical that is not peer-reviewed, how reliable/credible is the source? (See the "credibility check" at the end of this section.) If the source is a book, what can be determined about the publisher? A university press indicates a peer-reviewed, academic source. Other publishers, such as the press that produced this book (Routledge), can be looked up easily in order to discover what other kinds of texts they publish.

6. Throughout this process, take thorough notes. When reading hard copies, we ditch the highlighter in favor of a pencil. Underlining points, circling key terms, and writing margin notes are more active tasks than high-lighting. Interacting directly with the text on the page helps with reten-tion of information, more thoughtful use of the material, and more sophisticated insights. When using digital sources or library books, take notes, with page and paragraph numbers, in a reading journal. That is helpful not only for efficiently referring back to sources, but also for keeping track of your thinking on a topic over time and how it evolves with each new piece of information. One strategy for fruitful notetaking is to write down what was most exciting, convincing, doubtful, and/or confusing about each article or book chapter, as well as what questions it raised. Engaging with the text and asking questions about it are essential aspects of joining the community of scholars in the field.

7. Keep meticulous records of bibliographic information (author, article title, journal title, name of the database, date of publication, date of access, and page numbers) in the research journal. Most of that information can be cut and pasted right into a draft bibliography. As too many of us know, unearthing that information later is frustrating work!

8.   Learn the citation style expected for the literature review and use it in all notes and drafts. Scholars of dance history and theory usually use Chicago or Turabian (a variation of Chicago) style. Dance educators and dance therapists use APA (American Psychological Association). Getting into the practice of citing the research sources in the correct form from the very beginning will save you time in reformatting later, as well as instill the citation rules in a hands-on, timely manner.

Checking the credibility of sources

Conduct a *credibility check* on the sources that are not from peer-reviewed journals or book publishers. You should be able to answer "yes" to the following questions:

1.   Is the article free of errors in spelling and grammar? Do the vocabulary and sentence structures seem appropriate for academic research purposes?
2.   Is the author or sponsoring organization identified? Is the author qualified? Is the author affiliated with an accredited university, a nonprofit organization, or a government agency? (Qualifications and affiliations should be clearly identifiable.)
3.   Is there documentation for the information provided, in citations and a bibliography?
4.   Is the information verifiable in other sources?
5.   If the article is from a website, can the purpose of the site be determined (e.g., nonprofit advocacy, business/marketing, objective information/reference, for-profit news, personal soapbox)? Is that purpose seemingly objective? (In other words, it should not be overtly trying to sway readers to a particular opinion or to purchase a product.)
6.   Does it include a publication date or "last updated" date? Is it current?
7.   If a website, does it contain its own substantive content, as opposed to mainly providing links to other sites?
8.   Are links accurately described and still working?

Organizing the content of a literature review

As stated at the beginning of this chapter, a literature review is an *organized* discussion of published works. It does not follow the order in which the researcher found or read each source; that would be a reading journal—not particularly helpful to anyone besides the researcher. And literature reviews are rarely organized in chronological order, beginning with the oldest publication and moving forward in time or beginning with the most recent and moving backward. It only makes sense to organize a literature review chronologically when showing the changing trends in the area of study is critical to your research. For example, a study of Butoh in Japan may need to examine how that innovative form of dance theatre emerged from the collaboration of its founders as well as from the devastation of World War II. In such a case, a researcher could order the literature review from the oldest research to the most recent (or vice versa, as the case demands) and make clear that the sequential development is critical to one's understanding of the topic of study.

Most literature reviews, however, are organized thematically, around a few main ideas. Strong transitions between each main idea show how one relates to another, such as how new methods evolved from previous ones or how scholars in different parts of the world or from different schools of thought pursued similar questions in markedly distinct ways. How does one: (a) identify a few main ideas from many disparate sources; and (b) create transitions between them when they appear to be only loosely related? The strategy for accomplishing both of those complex tasks is to start grouping sources—and, usually, parts of different sources—at the time of reading. We recommend starting with big categories of the matters most often discussed in literature reviews: methods, findings, implications, and key characteristics of studies (anything in addition to the main methods, findings, and implications that stand out, such as a national study conducted in a very small country or the timing of data collection immediately after a major event that could reasonably be thought to influence results).

Organizing in a table or spreadsheet

As experienced researchers read and take notes on the literature, they also start to organize their sources, such as in a table or spreadsheet, which helps with subsequent tracking of patterns and relationships among the sources. Table 2.1 is an example of a table you might use to jot down salient elements of a few sources.

By jotting down key characteristics, methods, findings, and implications of each source, you can identify noteworthy contrasts as well as similarities. For example, the two or three sources that used *mixed methods* (a mixture of qualitative and quantitative methods, which is explained in Chapter 5) when most other published research on the topic has relied on quantitative data exclusively, could be discussed together in the literature review; or studies that came to vastly different conclusions could be juxtaposed for contrast.

Organizing in narrative form or bullet points

Some researchers prefer writing notes about each source in narrative form or in bullet points and then coding their notes for themes, patterns, and key differences. *Coding* in this instance refers to using different color highlights and/or different symbols (e.g., double underlining, asterisks) to mark patterns in a set of notes. For example, every mention of study subjects who are young children is highlighted yellow, while every mention of subjects who are adolescents is highlighted green. Or opposing findings are marked with left and right angled brackets (<, >).

TABLE 2.1 Literature review notes

Authors	Pub. date	Key characteristics of the study	Method and/or measures	Findings	Implications and my evaluation

The following questions may serve as prompts for the narrative or bulleted notes for each source:

- Is the significance of the author's work convincingly demonstrated?
- What are the author's theoretical approaches and/or research methods?
- What are strengths and/or limitations of the author's research methods? Was the study designed well?
- What are the main findings and their implications?
- Are the author's analysis and conclusions convincing?
- In what ways does the author's work contribute to the field of study?
- What are the article's or book's overall strengths and limitations?
- How does the work relate to your study?

Moving from notes to draft

Whether in a table, highlighted jottings, annotated bullet points, or other format, your organized notes about the research literature will help lead to the identification of patterns or other categories of information, known as *themes*. Each of the themes that emerges can become a paragraph or series of paragraphs of the literature review. Organizing the discussion of the research literature by themes highlights connections among the works under review. Such organization also demonstrates to the audience that you have conducted reflective and thoughtful research that has led to intriguing insights.

For it is your organized evaluation and analysis of the various sources' methods, evidence, findings, limitations, etc. that will give the literature review shape as an interesting argument. You will bring the research literature to life, so to speak, by moving well beyond summarizing key studies and even beyond noting some patterns. By organizing the literature review and choosing which sources to group with which, and explaining how sources evolve from and/or dispute one another, you can make a unique set of claims about the literature on your topic of inquiry.

A well organized, analytical literature review sets the stage for what comes next: the questions to be examined in, or the goal of, your study. For that reason, the conclusion of the literature review is the most important part. The last paragraph establishes where the existing literature leaves off and the present research proceeds. It demonstrates the need for the present study and what it will contribute to current knowledge.

Questions for discussion

1. Is a literature review important for all projects?
2. How do literature reviews vary by subject area?
3. How do you know if your literature review is sufficient?

3

CHOOSING TOPICS AND FORMULATING APPROPRIATE RESEARCH QUESTIONS OR PROJECT GOALS

Jenny Olin Shanahan

Summary

This chapter discusses the importance of formulating a research question that is unanswered, yet answerable—or a project goal that is original, yet doable—and the processes that could be used to pursue either one. It is essential that the development of research questions and refining of a project goal occur after, and are informed by, a thorough literature review. Many times, undergraduate students' initial suggestions for topics are much too broad in scope, and a literature review would quickly reveal this. An example would be the topic "best ways to teach ballet." Conversely, it is problematic when students' ideas are too narrow in scope, such as here: "What are the most common injuries sustained by adolescent female dancers?" If a question can be answered definitively or fairly quickly, it is not appropriate for a study. Occasionally, when students are formulating a research question or project goal, they communicate with a professor outside of dance, who can offer a different perspective. Such co-mentorship broadens the base of expertise from which students can draw.

Brainstorming topic areas

In order to generate ideas for a topic that is focused, timely, and of keen interest in your field of study, brainstorm responses to the following questions:

1. What are some interesting topics of conversation among you and your friends that relate to being a dancer, studying dance for your major, and/or pursuing a career in dance?

2. On the other hand, what topics rarely discussed by your friends seem significant to you?
3. Are there any dance trends that you have embraced or resisted?
4. Do you disagree with the "conventional wisdom" on a particular philosophy, practice, or stance in the field of dance?
5. Have you recently come to value something in your studies that had not previously seemed important to you?
6. Where are many people in your field of study going wrong (in your humble opinion)?
7. What are you most interested in learning about or contributing to in your intended career?

Refining the topic

Starting with a broad topic area when embarking on a scholarly project is common and perfectly acceptable. You might begin with general interest in an area of study, such as how innovations in technology are changing choreography, why Russian ballet stands out from other countries' contributions, or what makes early-childhood dance lessons most effective. You might even think that if you are taking on a long-term research project of a whole semester or more you will need a large topic to sustain the work all that time. Ironically, however, the opposite is usually true. A significant, long-term research study requires a specific, focused question. Getting the scope of that question right is the most valuable task to accomplish early in the research process.

The preliminary research and brainstorming you put into refining the topic is well worthwhile because, as we and our colleagues have seen repeatedly with our students' research (not to mention our own scholarly work!), the scope of the question can make or break the project. Imagine trying to carry out a comprehensive study of how technological innovations are changing choreography. Within that broad topic area there are dozens of possible approaches. For example, would it be a study about digitized dance notation? E-tracers in dance shoes? Wearable tech that provides new views of movements? Is it a philosophical exploration of what makes choreography a creative "human" enterprise when online movement banks can be utilized to select stock movements?

As would be the case for that example of using movement banks in choreography, topics that are too broad can cause frustration and lead to wasted time. If it turned out you were most interested in the philosophical debate about who is the choreographer when a piece is composed entirely from movement banks which were populated by several choreographers, you would likely be reading some theories about the role of crowd-sourcing and technology in human creativity, rather than, say, studying the problems with defining dynamics and phrasing when using digital software. Each of those approaches is significant and time-intensive in its own right. Skipping around multiple areas of a broad topic area results in a shallow and/or chaotic exploration. The clearer your focus, the more efficiently you can use your time and resources to conduct an in-depth, well-informed study.

Using the literature review and plenty of time to focus the question

Your review of the literature, as well as conversations with your professors, peers, and perhaps external experts, will allow you to understand what others have said about the topic and, in the process, help focus and refine your area of inquiry. By posing questions, analyzing the problem, and imagining various solutions, you will come to a deeper, more thorough comprehension of what is at issue and how to address it most effectively. This period of refining the topic into a strong, focused research question or project goal will be most valuable and satisfying if you give yourself adequate time and reflective space, as well as permission to scrap some ideas and begin again.

Very few scholars arrive at a perfectly refined question or goal through a singular epiphany. Most of us, most of the time, have to wallow around in half-formed ideas, mistaken directions, and—most frustrating of all—pursuits that have to be abandoned after days or even weeks of seemingly wasted work. Rather than fearing or trying to avoid "wasted" time—and, as a result, ending up with a simplistic or otherwise ineffectual project—try to see this time as an essential and valuable part of the process of creatively and comprehensively addressing a complex issue. If you are truly confronting a focused, significant, and problematic question—one with no single, agreed-upon solution—you will need to invest in a few good stumbling-around periods.

Guiding questions for refining a topic

Taking time for focusing and refining your question or goal does not need to be wasted time; in fact, it can be time incalculably well spent, particularly if you are engaging some critical, foundational questions:

1.   Why is the topic or question important? To whom is it important? Are particular groups of people affected more than others?
2.   What gives the topic tension? What would draw audiences to learning more about it?
3.   Read at least five current (i.e., usually published in the last five years) research articles about your topic and imagine yourself as a participant in a dialogue with the authors of the articles. What are the questions you would ask them? What seems to be missing or undervalued?
4.   What are the sources of the problem or need? Complex questions usually have complex webs of potential causes. Can you identify some of the strands of that web? Do you know professors or outside experts who can help?

5. What is the history or broader context of the topic? To get a handle on the context of your topic area, use reliable, general resources available through many college and university library websites, such as the *Oxford Dictionary of Dance* or the *International Encyclopedia of Dance*, which includes biographies of dancers and choreographers, social and cultural dimensions of dance history, and sections dedicated to myriad forms of dance, from folk and traditional to theatrical and sacred.

6. What other subject areas is your topic part of or related to? Might those other areas provide additional perspectives and/or interdisciplinary possibilities for research?

7. Why do you care about the topic area? What is its connection to your personal experiences or interests? In what ways does the interest extend beyond yourself, to other scholars and professionals in the field?

8. Who is the principal audience you want to reach with your research results? What do you want the audience to do as a result of your research: adjust their thinking about the issue; change some aspect of their practices/work/activities; provide support (e.g., funding, advocacy); experience something new?

Freewriting

Write down your responses to these questions and other ideas that come to you. Writing is the best way to reach clarity and insight about the issue you are exploring. Instead of trying to brainstorm only in your mind, we strongly recommend putting pen to paper or fingers to keyboard and *freewriting* your ideas for at least ten minutes at a time. Do not suppress any ideas even if they seem flawed, and do not edit for correctness. The kinesthetic act of writing (moving a pen across paper or typing on a keyboard), along with the mental "unblocking" of ideas, lead to insights that simply do not arrive if you stare at a blank screen or a piece of paper. Freewriting is a wonderfully simple and highly effective means of getting past "writer's block" or just getting off the "starting block" of any writing task.

Professor Peter Elbow, who has defined the drafting and revision process for college students for decades, explains the process of freewriting in his classic 1973 text *Writing without Teachers*:

> The idea is simply to write for ten minutes (later on, perhaps fifteen or twenty). Don't stop for anything. Go quickly without rushing. Never stop to look back, to cross something out ... to wonder what word or thought to use, or to think about what you are doing. If you can't think of a word or a spelling, just use a squiggle or else write, "I can't think of it." Just put down something.
>
> *(Elbow, 1973, p. 1)*

Freewriting allows you to get past your own internal critic and tap into sub-conscious, creative ideas that are difficult to access any other way (Boice, 1993). Such active brainstorming will produce a lot of material—plenty to throw out eventually, but also some rich ore that you may not have uncovered without journaling. The added bonus: you have notes for writing a first draft later. Even decades into our academic careers we use this freewriting strategy at the outset of new projects and when writer's block hits. Something almost magical often occurs at about the ten-minute mark of freewriting: a breakthrough of an exciting idea, more clarity about a muddled topic, or the concept for a new and better direction.

Topic areas in dance

UR in dance often takes the form of one of the following broad areas. (Many more possible topics can be found in Chapters 10–18.)

1. *Dance history*
2. Examples: social implications for dance of the percussive beats by Clive Campbell (Kool DJ Herc); ballet's transition to a performance art in the 18th century; impacts of the classical Indian dance Bharathanatyam
3. *Dance notation*
4. Examples: how Stepanov's notations helped bring Russian ballet to the Western world; Motif Notation's innovations of Labanotation
5. *Dance choreography*
6. Examples: writing a score for an improvisational dance group; re-composing a canonical ballet (e.g., Sleeping Beauty) for a small stage
7. *Dance education*
8. Examples: practices for teaching dance to children who are hearing-impaired; using dance to teach anatomy and physics
9. *Dance technology*
10. Examples: experiments in computerized notation systems; integrating virtual environments into dance performances
11. *Dance therapy*
12. Examples: clinical uses of dance for survivors of sexual abuse; effects of ballroom dance on Alzheimer's patients
13. *Cultural studies in dance*
14. Examples: using dance as political action; studying the moving body as both fixed and fluid representation of culture and identity; examining dance representations of AIDS

As each of the examples indicates, UR in dance invites you to explore something different from what has been done in the past. It absolutely should be something uncertain, risky, or challenging—something that takes you from familiar practices and assumptions to new and surprising ones. Of course trying something uncertain, risky, or challenging can be daunting and uncomfortable, but it is essential to an interesting and purposeful study.

Designing a research study or project goal

Investing time in focusing and refining your topic of inquiry undoubtedly helped you to revise your research question or project goal. You are ready to develop and carry out your plan, including creating a timeframe and figuring out logistics.

Will you be working with human participants in your research? Will you be distributing a survey, conducting interviews or focus-group discussions, recruiting volunteers, or asking people to try a particular intervention? If your answer is "yes" to any of those questions, or if you are otherwise interacting with people online or in-person (other than your professors or librarians) for any part of your research, you need approval or exemption from your university's Institutional Review Board (IRB). See Chapter 4 about research involving human participants. In the meantime, for the sake of planning your research, be sure to build in time to write an IRB application, have it reviewed, and to make any amendments to your research that the IRB could require.

Freewrite/brainstorm responses to the following questions to help you design your plan:

1. If people will be involved in your research (survey-takers, interviewees, etc.), what is your goal for the "sample size" (number of people to recruit)? What are their key characteristics (e.g., college students majoring in science, technology, engineering, and mathematics [STEM], people who learned ballet in their adult years, audience members at a particular dance performance)? How will you recruit the participants you need? How will you reduce bias in your sample?
2. How will your study be different from what has been done by previous scholars (especially if it is similar to research in the literature)?
3. How does your study reflect "best practices" in the field, promote diversity and inclusion, and engage with timely and significant matters?
4. Is your question or goal large enough that it should be broken into two or three parts? "Unpacking" a research question or project goal into two or more stages can help to organize your timeline as well as your eventual research paper. For example, assessing the effectiveness of a dance outreach program could involve the following facets: (a) surveys of the audiences; (b) interviews with the organizers; (c) focus groups with the dancers. Each could be written up separately, followed by a summation paper bringing all three together.

Organizing a timeline

Such brainstorming and figuring out the parts of your project design can lead to creation of an organized timeline. Table 3.1 is set up for a two-semester thesis. Of course yours should account for the time you have for your particular study. Keep adding to it as you realize additional facets of the project.

TABLE 3.1 Two-semester timeline

What do I need to do in the next week?	2–3 weeks from now (dates:)	4–6 weeks from now (dates:)	2–3 months from now (dates:)	3–6 months from now (dates:)	6–8 months from now (dates:)

Purpose statements

In many forms of academic research, scholars state the purpose of their study or project in one or two sentences. Stating directly and succinctly the purpose of your study clarifies it for yourself at the outset, as well as for your future readers. After the purpose statement, state the research question or questions that will be guiding your study.

Example 1: The purpose of this study is to …
    Guiding the design of this study are the following questions: …

Example 2: This research project examines …
    The following questions determined the focus of the research: …

Briefly articulating your study's purpose and identifying a manageable number of research questions or goals of the project can keep you on task. Write down your purpose and most critical questions/goals and post them at your work space. Just about any study can easily mushroom into an overly ambitious project, particularly if you are doing a good job of reading related literature and considering multiple perspectives. Having the parameters of your study posted right in front of you may help you to resist the temptation to totalize—to take on more than you can reasonably investigate, at least for now, in the attempt to be comprehensive.

Additional mentors

There are many specialty areas and subdisciplines in dance, including all the common dance genres (e.g., ballet, tap, jazz) in which different professors have expertise. Therefore, students can usually find certain professors who have an interest in the topic they are planning to research. Even if professors with the right expertise are not your instructors, one of them might be interested enough in the topic to be an additional mentor, or might have a project already in progress that could benefit from the assistance of an undergraduate researcher.

Interdisciplinary student projects particularly lend themselves to more than one faculty mentor. *Interdisciplinary* describes work that emerges from more than one academic discipline's knowledge base, research methods, ways of knowing (or *epistemologies*), and scholarly values. The two or more disciplines shape the work together, resulting in an approach and findings that could not be achieved through a single disciplinary perspective. Consider, for example, the interdisciplinary fields of dance education and dance therapy; for research in those areas, students need expert guidance not only from dance professors, but also from scholars who know about educational principles or psychotherapy, respectively. One of the examples of dance therapy research topics provided above, *clinical applications of dance for survivors of sexual abuse*, came from a student project that was co-mentored by faculty members in dance and psychology. The psychology professor was also a clinician who worked with children and adolescents who had experienced sexual abuse. Her expertise, as well as her access to research participants, were essential to the study.

Will success be measurable?

The ways to measure success will vary greatly depending on the particular topic, but some components of success include whether or not the project allows you to make an *original discovery* of something you and your mentor did not fully expect to find; whether some *new knowledge* is created, even if that knowledge is different from the anticipated results; and whether the findings indicate an *advancement of the discipline*, even in a small way. Successful dissemination of results, covered in depth in Chapter 9 of this book, is also a measure of success. Dissemination could be through a performance, presentation, and/or publication.

Questions for discussion

1. How do I know when I have a good research question?
2. When do I have to be sure of my topic and my research question?
3. What should be on the checklist for choosing a topic/question?

References

Boice, R. (1993). Writing blocks and tacit knowledge. *The Journal of Higher Education*, 64(1), 19–54.
Elbow, P. (1973). *Writing without teachers*. New York: Oxford University Press.

4

WORKING WITH HUMAN SUBJECTS

Jenny Olin Shanahan

Summary

The focus of this chapter is human subjects research. We define and discuss the role of the university Institutional Review Board (IRB) in reviewing, approving, and monitoring research involving human subjects, or human participants, in order to ensure that all research is conducted in accordance with federal, institutional, and ethical guidelines. We provide an overview of the Collaborative Institutional Training Initiative (CITI) training, including information for students about what to expect and a rationale for participating in the training. A brief synopsis of Rebecca Skloot's book *The Immortal Life of Henrietta Lacks* is included as a means of illustrating the far-reaching effects of unethical research methods, even when the researcher is well intentioned. The chapter concludes with a brief overview of types of dance research projects requiring IRB approval and CITI training.

Human subjects research

Any type of research that involves people—people who take a survey, people who are interviewed, people who participate in an experiment or study, etc.—is *human subjects research* or *human participants research*. A particular group of humans—what they think, how they change, what they do—is a subject of the research. Even if a very small part of the research includes people, even if the people are minimally consulted, and/or even if only one or two people are affected, the rules of human subjects research apply. For example, a study of common injuries among dancers that surveys some dancers about the injuries they have sustained is human subjects research. A dance education project that involves observing a master teacher at work is human subjects research. And interviewing a choreographer about her creative process is human subjects research.

Human subjects or human participants?

The traditional term "human subjects" is still used in most training programs and US federal guidelines, including those governing research conducted by the Department of Health and Human Services. Since the 1980s, though, largely due to the work of those engaged in research into the AIDS epidemic, the term "human participants" has often been used to refer to the people involved in a research study of any kind (Bayer, 1995). When AIDS was first identified, those who had contracted the disease, especially gay men and people who had used intravenous drugs, were acutely vulnerable to social stigma as well as incarceration. Homosexuality was considered a crime in over half of the states in the United States, was a disqualifier for teaching jobs and military service, and was often used as grounds for taking away parental rights. AIDS researchers needed to take thorough care not only to protect identifying information of patients, but also to ask questions with keen sensitivity and without apparent judgment regarding patients' sexuality or drug use. "In a remarkable and quite unusual process, all the more striking since it occurred during the conservative Reagan years, representatives of gay organizations entered into a complex set of negotiations over the nature of the confidentiality protections that were to be afforded to AIDS research subjects" (Bayer, 1995, para. 12). Together, leaders of gay rights organizations and medical researchers established standards for informed consent that effectively changed the role of AIDS patients in the research process from *subjects* to *participants*.

A *participant* is an active and willing member who is voluntarily contributing to the work, while the term *subject* implies passivity—the person on whom research is conducted. Research involving humans is vastly different from research conducted on more easily observable and controllable subjects such as plants and even mice. The main difference lies in humans' ability and right to choose what they do and what is done to them. Humans must be fully informed about research in which they participate, so they can either consent or not to the study.

Informed consent

Informed consent is fundamental to conducting research with humans that is legal and ethical. As bioethicist Jessica De Bord (2014) explained, informed consent traditionally refers to the process by which a competent adult agrees to, or refuses, a medical procedure, based on thorough understanding of the reasons it is being recommended and its potential benefits and risks. Informed consent originates in the legal and ethical rights of adults to determine what happens to their own bodies (De Bord, 2014). Informed consent laws now extend far beyond medical procedures to all forms of research or intervention involving people. People can benefit from and be harmed by a much broader realm of research than that involving medical procedures. Imagine for a moment a psychological study that could trigger Post Traumatic Stress Disorder (PTSD) in some subjects/participants. Because myriad forms of research involving human beings have the potential for harm, no

matter how seemingly minor, ethics and federal laws require that people participating in surveys, questionnaires, research observations, focus groups, interviews,
oral histories, and any other form of research give informed consent to participate.

The Immortal Life of Henrietta Lacks

The 2010 book by Rebecca Skloot, *The Immortal Life of Henrietta Lacks*, was
researched for over a decade to bring to light the far-reaching consequences and
injustices of unethical research practices. It is about a:

> poor black tobacco farmer whose cells—taken without her knowledge in
> 1951—became one of the most important tools in medicine, vital for devel-
> oping the polio vaccine, cloning, gene mapping, *in vitro* fertilization, and
> more. Henrietta's cells have been bought and sold by the billions, yet she
> remains virtually unknown, and her family can't afford health insurance.
>
> *(Skloot, 2010, back cover)*

Used across the United States as a first-year student convocation and summer
reading book, it won many awards including the 2010 *Chicago Tribune* Heartland
Prize for Nonfiction, the 2010 Wellcome Trust Book Prize, and the American
Association for the Advancement of Science's Award for Excellence in Science
Writing. Over 60 book critics named it as one of the best books of the year
(Skloot, 2018). "It's a story inextricably connected to the dark history of experi-
mentation on African Americans, the birth of bioethics, and the legal battles over
whether we control the stuff we're made of" (Skloot, 2010, back cover). The
compelling story of Henrietta Lacks provides undergraduate researchers an example
of why human "subjects" need to be informed, consulted with, and treated fairly
when involved in research studies. Even if your study does not involve human
subjects, the whole topic of ethics in research methods is something with which
you as a researcher should be familiar. Just about every area of research holds some
ethical considerations, even if not as directly as the research conducted on Henrietta Lacks.

Research that appears to have absolutely no risk of harm and/or may even
benefit participants is not off the hook from informed consent and ethical review.
Informed consent means people are agreeing or declining to participate *with full
knowledge*, even when there are no known risks either way. Informed consent also
includes people agreeing or declining to participate in research that may benefit
themselves or others. Why would anyone decide not to answer a short survey for a
professor's research if they did not have to provide their name, could take the
survey during class time (so would not have to use free time to do so), and would
receive extra-credit points for turning it in? The answer is, it doesn't matter. Each
of us has the legal right to opt in or out of participating in research without
explaining our reasons. Informed consent ensures that people are making the
decision with knowledge about what they are agreeing to or declining.

IRB approval

How do researchers know that they have provided enough information to participants to meet the legal standard of informed consent? How do we guard against unintentionally harmful or ethically questionable research practices? The primary gatekeepers protecting human participants from potential harm or manipulation, and preventing researchers from making ethical or legal violations (even inadvertently), are members of the IRB. Every institution in the United States in which research involving humans is conducted—every college and university, research hospital, school district, and other any other type of research facility—has, by law, a committee typically known as the IRB. Other countries have similar ethics boards that go by different names, such as Canada's Tri-Council (made up of representatives of three major granting agencies), the United Kingdom's Research Ethics Committee (REC), and the European Union's Ethics Committee. The 1964 "Declaration of Helsinki" by the World Medical Association established international ethical guidelines for research involving human subjects (World Health Organization, 2001).

According to US federal law, an IRB is made up of at least five experts in biomedical and social-behavioral research ethics. Members of the IRB are charged with protecting the rights and welfare of human subjects/participants in research conducted by anyone affiliated with the institution, including faculty, staff, and students of a college or university. The IRB must review and approve all research involving humans before the research may commence. The chairperson of the IRB is responsible for posting readily accessible (usually online) information about ethical and legal requirements for research involving humans, training sessions for researchers, and the IRB review process.

The IRB review process involves the main researcher, known as the *principal investigator* (PI)—usually the faculty member overseeing the undergraduate research—and the *co-investigator(s)*, who are the student(s) and anyone else collaborating on the research (e.g., community partners or faculty colleagues of the PI). The PI submits the IRB application and is ultimately responsible for ensuring that the research is carried out in accordance with what is described in the application, after it has been approved. None of the research involving human subjects/participants can begin before IRB approval—not even recruitment of the participants.

In addition to requiring a description of informed consent, IRB applications call for the following explanations:

1. How the PI and co-investigators will protect the privacy and confidentiality of all human participants
2. How the participants will be recruited
3. How the participants will be compensated, if applicable
4. Where the participants' confidential and/or identifying information will be stored (e.g., on a password-protected hard drive and/or a locking file cabinet)—and who will have access to it

5.   How the PI and co-investigators will dispose of confidential and/or identifying information after the study is complete and a certain period of time has passed (e.g., by fully deleting computer files and shredding paper records). Note that IRBs often require the PI to retain records in a secure location for a set period of time, typically three years, after the completion of the study

If the study includes a survey, a final copy of the survey must be attached. If the study includes interviews, oral histories, and/or focus groups, a list of questions to be asked—often known as the *interview guide* or *protocol*—must be attached. Researchers must stick to the questions on the interview guide, though related follow-up questions are permissible.

The IRB may require revision of the research protocol or even reject the application if required information is missing or incomplete, or if the board determines that the risks of the research are too great. The risks of research are highest when *vulnerable or protected populations* are involved; vulnerable populations include children, people in prison, and people with cognitive impairments, to name a few.

Why is training on human subjects research necessary?

Most US college and university IRBs require everyone conducting research with human subjects/participants to complete human-subjects research training every three years. That requirement includes undergraduate researchers. The training is provided by the CITI, which offers several different online courses and modules. Everyone involved in human subjects research takes the Responsible Conduct of Research CITI course and/or the Human Subjects Research CITI course, which has a Social-Behavioral-Educational track. Additional modules or courses may be required depending on the nature of the research.

Requiring researchers to take online CITI courses and pass the quizzes helps colleges and universities to ensure that research conducted in their name and with their support is done so with ethical integrity. Those who have completed CITI training are much more likely to carry out their research legally and ethically. They are informed about appropriate research protocols and the reasons for particular rules.

Completing training in human subjects research confers benefits on the researchers themselves, beyond the knowledge they gain about ethical research practices. Practically speaking, completing CITI training dramatically decreases the chance that a researcher will submit an IRB application that gets rejected or requires revision. Having to re-submit an IRB application requires extra time and can cause stress for the researchers. It can significantly delay the start of the study, sometimes for weeks, as protocols need to be rewritten and then reviewed again by the IRB. (At a large university, waiting a month or more for a decision from the IRB is not unusual.) Students working within the confines of a semester have no time to waste. Another benefit of completing CITI training is having ethics-course certification among your experiences—a distinctive credential for your résumé and/or graduate-school applications.

How do I get trained?

The IRB chairperson will let the PI know if CITI training is required for the planned research and, if so, which courses need to be taken. Each CITI course takes a few hours, but does not need to be completed in one sitting.

If you need to complete CITI training you will not need to pay for the courses. Each college and university has a CITI subscription that covers faculty, staff, and students of the institution.

Before creating an account on the CITI website, find out from the IRB chairperson how your institution handles student registrations and which courses you need to complete. Most likely you will be directed to create an account at https://www.citiprogram.org/index.cfm?pageID=22 by entering the name of your institution.

After each course module you will be quizzed on its content. The score considered "passing" is set by the IRB. (At our respective universities, the passing score is 80%.) Of course, you need a passing score to receive certification of completion.

Questions for discussion

1. What will happen if I don't take the appropriate steps to protect the rights of participants in my study?
2. How do I know what type of training is necessary?
3. Will CITI training help me after I graduate?
4. How do I choose my participants?

References

Bayer, R. (1995). AIDS, ethics, and activism: Institutional encounters in the epidemic's first decade. In R. E. Bulger, E. M. Bobby, & H. V. Fineberg (Eds.), *Society's choices: Social and ethical decision-making in biomedicine*. Washington, DC: National Academies Press. Retrieved from https://www.ncbi.nlm.nih.gov/books/NBK231965/

De Bord, J. (2014). *Informed consent. Ethics in medicine*. Seattle, WA: University of Washington School of Medicine. Retrieved from http://depts.washington.edu/bioethx/topics/consent.html

Skloot, R. (2010). *The Immortal Life of Henrietta Lacks*. New York: Crown Publishers.

Skloot, R. (2018). Retrieved from http://rebeccaskloot.com/the-immortal-life/press/

World Health Organization. (2001). Declaration of Helsinki. *Bulletin of the World Health Organization*, 79(4), 373–374. Retrieved from http://www.who.int/bulletin/archives/79(4)373.pdf

5

COLLECTING DATA

Jenny Olin Shanahan

Summary

This chapter explains the importance of sound research methods and creative processes. It introduces students to qualitative and quantitative methods and when to use one or the other, as well as when to mix methods. Examples of major data-collection strategies for undergraduate research (UR) in dance, including conducting library research, exploring primary sources, recording one's own observations with research journals and field notes, distributing surveys, and conducting interviews and focus groups, are illustrated. The main differences in methods between arts and humanities scholarship and social science research are described.

Importance of research methods

Research is a methodical investigation or inquiry aimed at answering a specific question or creating something new. The *methodical* approach is what gives a research study or creative project rigor and trustworthiness. After learning what is primarily known about the topic area through a review of the literature (see Chapter 2), scholars develop a focused and significant question or goal (see Chapter 3). As this chapter lays out, scholars then plan their own *methods* or *processes* for addressing the question or achieving the goal. They determine which sources of *data*, or information, would help to answer the question or achieve the goal and how to access those sources. Purposefully planning methods of data collection and carrying out the project according to that plan (as well as adapting the methods as needed, also based on thoughtful planning) are at the heart of conducting scholarly work.

The strength of a research study or creative project, therefore, depends most on its *methods*—the processes used to gather data/information and address the question or goal. Scholars who carefully select the methods best suited to the project set themselves up well for success. A successful study is not necessarily one in which the hypothesis or expected conclusion is proven, or in which the goal precisely comes to fruition, but one in which something new and interesting is discovered or created. That new and interesting discovery/creation is reached with sound methods or processes.

One of the common missteps we have observed in our mentoring of UR is a rush to decide on methods or processes that are obvious and readily accessible. We have had students who tried to rely entirely on secondary sources located through online research, for example, because they were most familiar with that method of information-gathering, even though additional sources of evidence would significantly strengthen their claims. And we have had to guide students away from simply conducting surveys of their peers as their primary research method; although gathering opinions from a group of friends, acquaintances, and/or classmates may be handy, that narrow group of people likely will not provide enough diversity of thought or richness of information to develop a full-fledged conclusion. This chapter is intended to guide student-researchers to more thorough, well planned methods—methods that are well aligned with the research question or goals of the project.

Sound methods are critical to the success of your entire project because the results depend on the quality of the data, and the quality of the data depends on the ways they were collected, recorded, and analyzed. Your process of gathering and analyzing the data must be made evident before your results are presented, in any dissemination of the work, such as a performance, conference presentation, or a research paper. The audience's trust in your findings will either be buttressed or undermined by how well you carried out the study and how well you explained carrying it out.

Establishing credibility as a researcher

Well-selected research methods—a careful process chosen precisely because it gets at the particular research question or project goal—lead to trustworthy results. In addition to setting up a successful project, sound methods give credibility to you as a researcher. For at least 25 centuries of human thought, the credibility of an author has been a foundation of effective argument, or *rhetoric*. In the fourth century BCE, the classical Greek scientist, philosopher, and teacher Aristotle explained that appealing persuasively to an audience requires *logos, pathos*, and *ethos*. Those three parts of a persuasive argument are now known as the *rhetorical triangle. Logos* refers literally to the *logic* of one's argument—the reasons, evidence, and explanation that convince others of one's points. *Pathos* concerns appeals to the audience by connecting with them through emotions and values. An example of *pathos* in a research paper about dances that seek to raise awareness about human trafficking is the inclusion of moving stories about some of the survivors of trafficking whose individual experiences were brought into the choreography. Statistics can be used as a form of *pathos* as well, such as by demonstrating how prevalent the often-hidden practice of human trafficking of immigrants in the United States actually is, perhaps stirring audience members' righteous anger about an ongoing crisis.

Ethos relates to the character of the writer/speaker. The importance of *ethos* to rhetoric/argument derives from the idea that audience members will only be persuaded by the logic of the claims (*logos*) and the appeals to their values (*pathos*) if they trust the person making the argument. That trust is established when those making claims explain with transparency how they arrived at their conclusions—in the case of research, how they gathered their data and why they went about it in the ways they did. If, on the other hand, the audience is not convinced of the credibility and quality of the work of the researcher, they have no reason to accept the claims.

Triangulated, intentional, and impartial data collection

Triangulation of data

Establishing your credibility as a scholar and ensuring, as well as possible, the success of your study require collecting data in *triangulated, intentional,* and *impartial* ways. *Triangulated data collection* refers to gathering information in a variety of ways as a system of data "checks and balances." Data from one source can be corroborated or disputed by a different source. When multiple sources of information are brought to bear on a research question, the researcher can attain a more reliable and comprehensive understanding. Consider for example a dance education study on the value of and best practices for teaching dance to children who are hearing-impaired. Multiple perspectives are needed on how to teach dance's visual and tactile cues to young children, whether and in which ways to include hearing and hearing-impaired children in the same class, and how to increase children's awareness of rhythm and vibration. Pursuing just one or two points of view would be insufficient for understanding the range of pedagogical approaches and underlying values related to the topic. Only by culling information from numerous sources and synthesizing it into a multi-faceted claim could a researcher on the topic arrive at an informed and insightful argument. That work of drawing from multiple sources is triangulation.

Although the term "triangulation" has led some of our students over the years to conclude that they need exactly three sources of information, the reality is more nuanced than that. The three legs of a simple camp-stool give it stability; take one away, and the stool topples over, but adding legs solidifies it. We prefer to think of triangulation in terms of that metaphorical camp-stool's overall stability rather than its literal three legs. In other words, triangulated research might require only three sources of information to stand solidly on its claims, but it may need more. Would you accept three examples of teaching dance to students with hearing impairments? If only the lessons of teachers who work with preschool-aged children were consulted, would you have a broad enough understanding of possible pedagogies for older students? What if pedagogical techniques used with hearing-impaired adolescents and adults taking their first dance classes were added for consideration? The research would certainly be more thorough and the findings more consequential.

Further triangulation could lead to entirely different types of research sources, such as those that explore broader "inclusion" (hearing and hearing-impaired children learning together) versus "pull-out" (special education focused on hearing-impaired students) class dynamics and teaching practices.

To plan triangulated methods, you might brainstorm about the various forms of data that could address your research questions (or parts of a single research question) or help you achieve your creative goals and then organize them into a table along the lines of Table 5.1.

Intentionality in data collection

Lest it sound as though more and more sources automatically make research better, we move to the second criterion of sound research methods: intentionality. *Intentional data collection* refers to the careful thinking involved in determining which sources to pursue. What types of data will allow you to gain the information you need? By selecting sources of information intentionally and then explaining why you collected data in the ways you did, you avoid a scattershot (random and overly general) approach to research. In the study of best practices of teaching dance to hearing-impaired students, for instance, intentionally choosing salient examples of teaching methods for preschool-aged as well as older students, and for inclusion and pull-out classes, would lead to a more complete understanding of various pedagogical approaches. Simply compiling example after example of how some teachers have adapted their pedagogy for hearing-impaired students would not be as effective as selecting key practices from rigorous case studies to arrive at evidence-based pedagogical interventions.

Avoiding bias and ensuring impartiality

The third expectation of credible researchers, *impartiality*, requires effort to reduce potential bias and errors. Biased or otherwise sloppy scholarship undermines the study itself as well as the credibility of the researcher. Bias in research comes in many forms, some of it unconscious on the part of the scholar. It might include preference for, or prejudice against, a particular outcome that leads to overemphasis (or ignoring) of certain results. If a researcher expects members of a focus group to be enthusiastic about a shared experience, the

TABLE 5.1 Triangulating data

Part 1 of Research Question/Goal	First Method of Data Collection for Question 1	Second Method of Data Collection for Question 1	Third Method of Data Collection for Question 1
Part 2 of Research Question/Goal	First Method of Data Collection for Question 2	Second Method of Data Collection for Question 2	Third Method of Data Collection for Question 2

researcher might glom on to a few stray comments that fit that expectation. On the flip side, if members of the focus group suspect the researcher is hoping for particular responses, they might accommodate that expectation, especially if they have a relationship with the researcher that would benefit from positive reinforcement. For those very reasons the best practices of focus-group research include having a neutral person facilitate and record the discussion, without the researcher even being in the room.

Similarly, the ways in which survey questions are worded may reveal the biases of the researcher and skew responses. Using validated survey instruments designed by researchers with expertise in survey design mitigates those tendencies toward unconscious bias. If you need to develop your own survey, we recommend studying the elements of good design, starting with guidelines for beginning survey researchers, such as Vannette's (2015) "10 tips for building effective surveys" and asking for feedback on your draft questions from professors who teach research methods.

Even peer-reviewed research articles are likely to reflect the values of the journals that publish them, so over-reliance on sources from one journal should be avoided. As these examples indicate, impartial research design requires vigilance. Consistently asking yourself how sources of data could be obtained with the least possibility for bias can lead to helpful ideas for fair and even-handed methods. Explaining in your method section the steps you took to reduce bias and the chance of errors demonstrates your impartiality and credibility as a researcher. Informed readers can and should be attentive to signs of prejudice and imprecision in reports of research. They will appreciate indications that you collected data carefully and as impartially as possible.

Quantitative, qualitative, and mixed methods research

How do you decide on the types of research data to triangulate, select intentionally, and collect impartially? One rough breakdown of the types of research data you might gather is *quantitative* and *qualitative*. *Quantitative data* is numerically measurable and reportable information. Quantitative data literally shows the calculable quantity or amount of something. Examples include the number or percentage of participants who gave a particular response to a survey question; the average increase in scores between participants' pretest and posttest; the amount of time needed to complete a series of tasks; and even the results of a structural analysis of the complexity of a piece of music.

Qualitative data cannot be measured numerically; it is descriptive information about the qualities of people's ideas or behaviors, or any other subject of study that requires interpretation rather than calculation. Examples of qualitative data include transcripts of interviews; open-ended written responses on surveys; analysis of the emotions expressed in a piece of dance; observations of people's behaviors described in field notes; and evaluations of athleticism, form, or choice of music for a dance.

Sources of information are rarely exclusively quantitative or qualitative; many can be analyzed in different ways for quantitative or qualitative data, such as pre and posttests that could be evaluated in terms of how many responses were correct (quantitative measure) and/or analyzed for patterns in the open-ended responses (qualitative interpretation). Likewise, researchers often benefit from obtaining both quantitative and qualitative data. Using both types of information to get at different facets of the research question is known as *mixed methods research*.

Quantitative methods

The following are the most common quantitative methods used by undergraduate researchers in dance:

- *Surveys/questionnaires with multiple-choice or Likert-scale responses*: surveys and questionnaires capture demographic and/or opinion data that are self-reported by individuals. A Likert scale is usually made up of five or seven choices aimed at measuring degrees of agreement, from strongly disagree to strongly agree, for example. A Likert scale provides a more nuanced set of responses than simple agree-or-disagree binary choices.
- *Tests of content knowledge, ability, attitude, or skill*: pretest and posttest data are often used to determine whether an intervention, such as a new teaching technique or a particular experience or event, may have affected participants' knowledge or attitudes. The pretest and posttest ask for the same information at different points in time—days, weeks, or months apart.
- Pre and posttests may be given to one group of participants to measure change over time, or distributed to two sets of participants known as the *experimental group* and *control group* in order to make a comparison between them. The experimental group participates in the intervention being studied ("the experiment"), such as a new method of teaching. The control group continues with the status quo. Experimental and control groups usually share basic demographics in common. A study aimed at determining whether self-learning Labanotation or learning it from a tutor is more effective could have one small group of students independently read Ann Hutchinson's *Labanotation* and write down their own simple choreography with the notations as they learn them, and have another group take a Directed Study course in Labanotation from an experienced Laban Movement analyst; both groups of students would demonstrate their skills in reading and using notation after a certain amount of time.
- *Structural analysis of dance notations, performance, or other "texts"*: a quantitative structural analysis entails some form of counting, such as the number of a type of notation in a choreographer's work or the words that came up most frequently on an online discussion board.
- *Statistical analysis*: the analysis of statistical data gathered by oneself or previous researchers is a sophisticated quantitative research skill. Statistical data include a

vast array of evidence, from individuals' personal/demographic information to immense sets of organizational and national information.

Qualitative methods

These are the most common forms of qualitative data in UR in dance:

- *Surveys/questionnaires with open-response questions*: open-response questions invite survey-takers to write out answers to questions that do not lend themselves to either-or or multiple-choice responses. They allow participants to convey a range of ideas, attitudes, and examples, often providing rich information for researchers. (Many surveys of course include both quantitative and qualitative questions.)
- *Interviews*: interviews, which are typically one-on-one interactions in which the participant answers a set of questions posed by the researcher/interviewer, may be audio-recorded with the permission of the participant. Whether the interview is recorded or not, the interviewer usually takes extensive notes during and immediately following the interview.
- *Focus groups*: focus groups are akin to group interviews. A group of people with something in common that is of interest to the researcher (e.g., students in a summer undergraduate-research program; attendees of the same concert; survey respondents who checked the box at the end of the survey indicating their willingness to be contacted for follow-up research) is invited to participate in a discussion about the topic. The group should be small enough that everyone can contribute a response to some or all of the questions—usually between five and 20 participants. The facilitator poses questions to the group and may either encourage a free exchange of responses or suggest a means of equitable participation. Focus groups may be audio-recorded with the informed consent of each participant. Often a note-taker accompanies the facilitator so that the facilitator can attend to the group dynamics without the additional task of writing notes.
- *Document analysis*: some student-researchers get the extraordinary opportunity to work with primary sources in an archive or more accessible online collection. *Primary sources* are original documents or artifacts created in the time period being studied, such as diaries/journals, original manuscripts and composition notes, letters and other correspondence, and video recordings. Archives around the world preserve original documents of historical and cultural significance in secure, fire-proof cabinets in temperature-controlled, low-humidity rooms, all to ensure that they will not be lost to current and future generations. University library archives, as well as many archives associated with museums, historical societies, and other public and private libraries, offer rich troves of primary sources for student-researchers. You may be required to get a brief training from the archivist and to wear archivist gloves—or you may have to view fragile, high-value pieces through plastic or glass—but those precautions are well worthwhile, as there is nothing quite like the thrill of working with a document written in a world-renowned choreographer's own hand.

- Digitized library and museum collections have made primary-source research possible from your own computer or your university's library database. Digital photos of documents and recordings of performances bring the archives right to you.

- Anything that interprets or is otherwise at a remove from a primary text (e.g., an article that includes excerpts of letters) is a *secondary source*. Your notes in a journal—capturing key quotations as well as your own textual analysis and observations—are invaluable sources of qualitative data. When reading and analyzing a text (whether in the form of choreography notation, a narrative text, a data table, or a piece of artwork, to name a few), you could be jotting down ideas that strike you, direct quotations you want to use and cite, questions that pop up in your mind, connections you see to other texts, and any number of other thoughts. Those notes, especially if you color-code them according to patterns and/or mark up significant details, is a form of qualitative data analysis.

- *Case study*: empirical observation and analysis of one important case (or small number of cases) may give deep insight into a broader issue. The "case" may be a person, course, event, or other phenomenon. A UR study on one participant's use of a modified wheelchair for dance could focus on the participant's feedback on ease of use, mobility, and control over several sessions of dancing while using the chair. Based on that participant's experience, the researcher could make some qualified suggestions about the pros and cons of particular wheelchair modifications for dance.

- *Observation* (also called *field observation* or *direct observation*): conducting observations on behaviors or other phenomena in a certain setting can be a valuable qualitative research method when carried out by rigorous researchers who are doing much more than simply watching. Observation research requires detailed field notes about what is observed—a crucial aspect of its methodological rigor. Sometimes the field notes are structured to include certain behaviors or participants while purposely ignoring others in order to focus on a predetermined set of data, such as observation research on how a particular choreographer works with dancers during rehearsals. Other field notes are open to everything that catches the researcher's attention, without a prediction of what to expect.

- If the observation is to be conducted covertly (without the knowledge and consent of those being observed), privacy must be protected, and the IRB will consider whether the research could be conducted effectively with informed participants instead. If the subjects/participants know they are being observed, the researcher must consider the Hawthorne Effect, the psychological phenomenon of people changing their behavior because they are being observed. Such decisions about covert or overt observations are usually discussed in the method section of a research paper.

- *Participant observation*: conducting observations on the behaviors of a group of people while involved with them over a period of time offers a more intimate angle on observation research. Examples of participant observation include student-teachers conducting research on middle-school students' learning of dance in their physical education (PE) class; a member of a dance troupe seeking to determine the most effectual practice techniques for small groups of dancers; and undergraduate researchers in dance reflecting on their own and their classmates' experiences in their capstone class as a means of informing future students, as they have done for this book. As with other forms of observation, participant observation requires detailed field notes, though the notes may have to be written immediately after the observation time because participating and note-taking simultaneously may not be possible.

Mixed methods

Some forms of research can be quantitative, qualitative, or mixed methods, depending on the types of information to be gathered. Two examples are as follows:

- *Longitudinal study*: empirical observation and analysis of something over a significant period of time (e.g., ten-year commitment to ballet after a particular form of instruction).
- *Pilot study*: collecting data about a new intervention or process while it is carried out for the first time, and analyzing the data to determine the intervention's longer term efficacy.

Note that IRB approval is required for all of these forms of research (quantitative, qualitative, and mixed methods) except when they do not involve people in any way. IRB approval is not required for use of *archival data*—information already collected by other researchers (who had IRB approval) that is now available, with no personally identifiable information, for new researchers to analyze.

Arts and humanities methods

You may notice that in some scholarly papers in the arts and humanities, research methods are discussed only briefly or may even be implicit (not explicitly identified). That occurs when the author is using a widely accepted method with which the intended audience would be familiar. An ethnographic study published in a journal dedicated to ethnography, for example, would omit some of the rationale for the selected method. For UR papers and presentations, however, the method should be made apparent, as the audience is rarely limited to narrow experts.

That said, you may also notice explanations of scholarly processes that are referred to in other terms. Many scholars in the arts and humanities would not use the word *method* to describe their process of collecting information, as it is traditionally associated with research that is *empirical* (verifiable by observation) or *experimental* (based on scientific tests). Much of the scholarly work conducted in the arts and humanities is *theoretical*: it builds on existing knowledge to explain or create new concepts/phenomena. Theoretical scholarship is distinct from empirical and experimental research in many ways, as indicated by the different terminology.

One of our students, for example, choreographed a dance that aimed to teach the processes of DNA replication and mutation to children with family members diagnosed with cancer. The work was theoretical as well as creative because it built on research on how DNA replication errors during cell division contribute to the spread of cancer. It also built on the student's training in choreography that allowed her to generate a new way of representing a complex biological process.

Scholars doing theoretical and creative work may or may not use the term "method" to describe their process. Alternative terms include "process," "technique," "approach" (including "theoretical approach" and "critical approach"), "study," and "analysis." The student who created the dance about DNA replication and mutation explained her "scholarly process" rather than her "research methods" because that terminology better fit her work. All of that is to say that various terms may be used in different contexts, but whatever phrasing is used, scholars are expected to describe the methods of their inquiries. In that student's case, she explained several parts of her scholarly process:

- Reading recent literature about DNA replication in order to understand the latest scientific information on DNA replication and mutation processes and how errors in replication can lead to cancer;
- Researching child-development literature on best practices for talking with children at various ages about difficult subjects, such as terminal illnesses with which they themselves or their family members have been diagnosed;
- Creating notations of dance movements that aim to represent DNA strands and mimic the processes of replication and mutation;
- Recruiting dancers and teaching them about the goals of the dance and the basics of DNA replication;
- Designing simple costumes for each dancer to wear a single color representing [word?] of DNA;
- Selecting and securing permission for a piece of accompanying music;
- Choreographing the dance based on notations and input from dancers;
- At rehearsals at various stages, consulting with cancer researchers about the accuracy of the biological representation and with early-childhood educators about the efficacy of communicating through the dance with young children;
- Writing introductory narrative information to accompany the performance.

Those methodical steps aligned with the student's goals for the project and demonstrated that she possessed the knowledge and ability to do the work.

Social science methods

Some scholarship in the field of dance, such as research in dance education and dance therapy, would be characterized as social science research, which is mainly *empirical* (verifiable by observation), though social scientists also conduct theoretical research. One of our students majoring in dance education conducted a research study during his student-teaching semester in a middle-school PE class. He hypothesized that sixth-graders who learned hip-hop dance techniques in PE over a four-week period (the experimental group) would be more engaged in PE than their peers in another PE class that followed the usual PE curriculum of team games and sports (the control group). The differences between the two classes were measured by the middle-school students' participation scores assigned by their respective PE teachers during the four-week period, as well as by pre and post surveys. The student's methods were *empirical* in that he could answer his research question mainly through observable evidence: the sixth-graders' survey responses and the PE teachers' assigned scores. His empirical methods included the following steps:

- Developing pre and post surveys from models in the research literature
- Working with his faculty mentor to complete the university's IRB application for ethics review (see Chapter 4)
- Obtaining informed consent of parents for their minor children to participate in the research study
- Distributing, recording, and analyzing student responses to pre and post surveys
- With the permission of the school principal and participating teachers, analyzing PE participation scores (without any identifying information) across two sixth-grade classes

As you can see in a comparison of the two students' main methods (choreographing a dance to "tell the story" of DNA replication and mutation, and studying the effects of incorporating hip-hop dance in a middle-school PE curriculum), each pursued a very different means of answering their research questions in the field of dance—just as each ought to. The student-teacher's question required an empirical approach that obviously would not work for a theoretical/creative project.

That study of the effects of learning hip-hop dance techniques on middle-school students' engagement in PE could also draw on movement theory, though, in which case the methods would include *theoretical* as well as empirical research. The student could analyze theories about the effects of rhythmic movement on the brain and draw connections to his own study. Building on existing knowledge about rhythmic movement affecting the brain would be a theoretical method.

Another way that social scientists conduct theoretical research is in the reverse order: rather than analyzing an existing theory and applying it to one's own work, researchers sometimes develop a new theory from their research findings. The term for that form of research is *grounded theory*. The new theory emerges from the "ground" up. A scholar may discover something through empirical research that is not explainable with existing theories. The discovery could be a fluke or a simple anomaly. But if the discovery can be replicated in a different context or otherwise leads to new understanding, the researcher might develop a grounded theory.

Organizing the method section of a social-science research paper

The scholarly methods or processes are usually explained in a paper after the introduction and the review of the literature. Many professors, journal editors, and other readers of your written work, especially in the social sciences, expect research papers to follow a standard format:

1. *Abstract*: a brief overview (anywhere from 60 to 250 words, depending on the particular guidelines provided) of the whole paper, with a focus on the methods, results, and implications of the research
2. *Introduction*: the purposes of which are to orient readers to the topic of inquiry and inspire interest in it
3. *Literature review*
4. *Method*
5. *Results*
6. *Discussion*
7. *Conclusion*: which typically offers next steps and implications of the research

Academic posters often include each of those sections as well, though the order may be moved around as needed for column space and visual appeal. Oral presentations may also cue the audience when moving to each section, to clarify distinctions between what came from the review of the literature, for example, as opposed to what was learned in the speaker's own research study.

Subsections of the method section

Within each of those sections researchers usually include *subsections* to delineate and organize further the points that go together within each section. Subsections are particularly helpful to aid the reader's understanding of long research papers. We focus here on typical subsections of a method section. The subsections of a literature review (see Chapter 2) and results and discussion sections (see Chapter 6) are unique to each paper because they emerge from the themes of the particular research study.

The method section of a research paper or poster, however, often includes three standard subsections, organized under their own subheadings:

1. *Participants*: a description of the human subjects/participants involved in the study and how they were recruited or observed, if applicable. In most cases, participants should not be identifiable. Typical information to provide about participants:

    - Number of participants, which may include the number recruited as well as how many actually participated, if applicable
    - Gender breakdown
    - Race and ethnicity breakdown
    - Range of ages and median age

2. Information particular to your participants should be included as well; e.g., "All participants were undergraduate students at a large public university in the southeastern United States."

3. This subsection could also describe briefly how participants were recruited; e. g., "Potential interview subjects were recruited by email, using contact information provided in the National Dance Education Organization (NDEO) National College Dance directory. The recruitment email introduced the researcher, summarized the purpose of the study, noted the university's IRB approval, and requested 30 minutes of the participant's time for an interview over Skype."

4. *Materials*: information about the things used to collect data and/or conduct measurements (e.g., surveys, timed tests, materials the participants read or watched on video). This subsection is termed *Apparatus* when the data were gathered through the use of technical equipment or research instruments (e.g., noise-canceling headphones, eye-movement tracking device, analytical software) or *Apparatus and Materials* if a mixture of mechanisms were used to collect data. Please note that this subsection may need a different subheading that more accurately captures what kinds of things were used to obtain information (e.g., *Survey Instrument* may be a better subheading than *Materials* if the only research material was a survey).

5. *Procedure*: an explanation of how the data were collected, verified, and analyzed. The procedure section usually includes a discussion of *variables*, or factors that can change and therefore could affect the results of the study. Consider for example a study of how freestyle dancing for ten minutes right before taking Calculus I exams might affect student performance on the exams. There are multiple variables to consider in such a study: how long each participant studied for the exam, the time of day of the exam, participants' degrees of enthusiasm or beliefs about dancing, etc. Rigorous research attempts to control for as many variables as possible, such as by selecting participants with similar self-reports about their attitudes about dancing and similar grades on previous exams. Any such attempts to limit the number of variables should be noted. Explain the variables that could not be controlled (e.g., participants' attitudes about dancing) and acknowledge how they could affect the results.

Variables that may weaken the results of the study are a form of *Limitations*. The limitations of your research methods should be acknowledged either as you discuss each method or in summary at the end of the method section.

While those three subsections are fairly standard, students are often not required to include them in exactly that way, nor to be limited to those three. In a paper on a complex research study, additional subsections are often needed to delineate aspects of the research methods.

Our students often ask us how much detail is needed in the method section. As you can imagine, anyone who has conducted a long, complicated research project could go on and on about each step of the process, but an exhaustive account would not be of interest or need to most audiences. A widely accepted consideration for the degree of detail in a method section is whether future researchers would have enough information to replicate the study in their own settings. One aspect of research is the reliability of results: the extent to which the results would be consistent if the study were carried out again with similar conditions. Reliability can only be tested if each researcher's methods are spelled out with enough clarity for others to run the investigation again. We recommend trying to strike a balance between presenting clear, replicable information about stages of your research process and not going into excruciating detail. Reading method sections of published papers in your topic area is the best way of understanding where that balance lies.

More about acknowledging the limitations of the research

Every research study has certain limitations: it is limited by the number of survey respondents, or the amount of time over which a change is studied, or the inherent bias of the researcher, just to name a few examples. Some limitations are unavoidable and expected.

When the limitations will undermine the results of your research, however, you need to use an alternative method of data collection. If the student-teacher studying middle-school students' engagement in PE incorporating hip-hop dance were to receive informed consent from only a small percentage of parents of students in the class, he would need to adjust his methods or add another form of data collection for triangulation. When the limitations are avoidable (such as when your presence in a focus group could prompt less-than-honest responses, and someone else could facilitate the focus group instead), you are expected to do your best to prevent them.

Unavoidable limitations that you anticipate ahead of time should be noted in the method section. What are the limitations in each form of data you are collecting? For example, were you only able to study one group of people (an experimental group) without a control group for comparison? Were there distortions in the digital video recording you analyzed? Was the single semester you had for your capstone project an insufficient amount of time to measure significant differences in pre and posttests? There is no need to document each and every imperfection in your research process; only the factors that likely weakened the project in noticeable ways need to be acknowledged.

Later, when you discuss the results (see Chapter 6) you can speculate on how some results may have been affected by the limitations.

Other means of organizing research methods

Earlier in this chapter we noted that various disciplines use different terms for *methods*, as well as different ways of organizing scholarly writing. Those differences are not arbitrary or accidental, of course. Each academic discipline is distinguished by its *epistemology*, or its theories and ways of knowing. Epistemology encompasses why and how people in a particular field of study gain knowledge: how we know what we know, which methods are used to teach and discover knowledge, which forms of evidence are considered valid, where knowledge originates, and where its limits might be. It stands to reason that scholars operating under different epistemologies would pursue new knowledge in divergent ways and therefore write and speak about their processes in divergent ways.

A good example of the different terminology reflecting different epistemologies is the word "procedure," which is particularly suited to empirical and experimental research. Scholars making empirical observations or running experiments must take great care with their research protocol, or procedure. To guard against bias in their observations, to measure accurately, to make equal comparisons, and for many other reasons, empirical and experimental researchers need to follow established procedures. They know that their results will only be meaningful if their data are collected and recorded in precise, methodical steps. Detailing their procedure in the method section of a research paper is understandably expected.

The procedures followed by theoretical and creative scholars are not usually so rigorous or clear-cut—nor do they need to be. A great deal of the scholarly work done in the arts and humanities is interpretive. There is no single, established procedure for analyzing a piece of dance, much less for choreographing one! Individual scholars take their own approaches to theoretical and creative projects, and those approaches are not necessarily linear or prescriptive. Creative projects in the arts, as well as many other fields, are notoriously ill-structured. We know a scholar of "pure mathematics" who studies concepts so abstract they have no real-world referents; when asked to describe her methods of constructing proofs she said simply, "I think about the problem for a really long time." Imagine explaining the procedure for that research method!

Students conducting scholarly work that does not fit the methods and terminology of empirical or experimental research have an array of options for describing their processes, including the following two, which could also serve as subheadings:

- *Research design*: a summary of the investigation (the research question/goal and a few objectives of the study) and the major stages of gathering information to address the question/goal. The stages of information-gathering may be organized *chronologically* (starting with the first step and concluding with the last) or *thematically* (clustering related steps together).

- *Theoretical approach* (also called *critical approach* or *methodological approach*): an explanation of the theory or theories that were foundational to the research and how that existing theory was applied to your own study. We recommend starting by summarizing the theory and then demonstrating its relevance to your research question or project goal. A theoretical idea may be used as a kind of lens for examining primary or secondary sources or other qualitative data; it may offer a methodological approach that you can adapt for your own investigation; and/or a theory may be brought into dialogue with other theories to create a richer understanding of the topic of study.

Questions for discussion

1. Are there standard ways to collect data in dance?
2. Which data collection methods are appropriate for my topic?
3. For a survey, how do I judge whether my sample size is appropriate?

Reference

Vannette, D. (2015). 10 tips for building effective surveys. Retrieved from https://www.qua
ltrics.com/blog/10-tips-for-building-effective-surveys/

6

ANALYZING AND SYNTHESIZING DATA

Jenny Olin Shanahan

Summary

The results or findings are the most substantive part of conducting research. This chapter outlines how research results and interpretation of those results are reported in different disciplines and types of papers and presentations. It provides prompts for freewriting or otherwise thinking about the implications of data. While a full exploration of qualitative and quantitative data analysis is beyond the scope of this text, this chapter includes fundamental information about the terms and techniques involved in analyzing different types of information. It discusses the importance of triangulating results, identifying overarching themes, and aligning the discussion of research results with the research question and the review of the literature. The chapter concludes with a reminder about acknowledging any limitations of the research that significantly affect the results.

Results and discussion

The *results* (or *findings*) of your study constitute what you have learned from the research process. The results include the data along with your analysis or interpretation of the data. Merely reporting the data is not enough. The point of research is the *analysis* and *interpretation* of what the data signify.

In most reports of scholarly work the results/findings are explained right after the methods/process. In APA-style, social-science papers, the *results* are reported separately from the *discussion*. The results section gives a basic explanation of the data, and the subsequent discussion section provides more thorough interpretation of the results and explains the wider implications of what was discovered. In papers and presentations in the arts and humanities, however, the results or findings are usually interpreted while they are reported. There is no divide between the results and discussion—or between the results and the researcher's interpretation and statement of implications.

Analyzing research data

Knowing the etymology (origin) of the verb *analyze* can be a useful means of understanding what is really called for when you are asked to analyze information. The Latin origin of *analysis* translates to the "resolution of anything complex into simple elements" (analysis, 2010). In that original concept of analysis as the breaking down of complex ideas, analysis is posited as the opposite of *synthesis*, which refers to putting parts back into a coherent whole. That idea effectively informs the task of data analysis, which is very much about breaking apart complex information into simpler parts. The Greek etymology of *analysis* adds another facet to this understanding: "a breaking up, a loosening, releasing"; the verb form in Greek is "to set free; to loose a ship from its moorings" (analysis, 2010). Imagine for a moment what that version of analysis might look like in undergraduate research. What would it mean to "loosen" or "release" research data? How does the image of a ship set free of its moorings represent something about the task of analyzing information? We consider the work of data analysis to be analogous to the Latin and Greek origins of the English word. Analysis is an act of setting free into the world the knowledge contained in quantitative and qualitative data. The analyzer's work of breaking the data apart helps others to make sense of the information. The researcher's analysis could even be described as loosening up the densely packed evidence, allowing others to see and understand the component parts.

Analysis is what gives meaning to the quantitative and qualitative data you have collected. The data do not hold meaning in and of themselves; it is your analytical work that translates for others what the information actually signifies. This chapter offers tools and techniques for doing that important work of making meaning from data.

Data analysis exercise

Examine each piece of data and freewrite answers to the following questions:

- What is interesting/exciting/notable about this piece of information?
- What is the story it can tell?
- Do you think this data-point misrepresents what is really going on?
- What, if anything, is disappointing about it?
- Is it consistent with anything you found in your review of the literature? Does it contradict anything you read in the research literature?
- How could it be most effectively presented? In narrative form? In tables or graphs? Key quotations? (Quotations may come from textual analysis, from research participants, from your own research journal, etc.)

Identifying themes in the data

The analysis of data is about figuring out the *implications* (or conclusions that can be drawn) of what was discovered. To help our students start to organize their research results we ask them to list and then freewrite about the three to five themes they have learned from their research (the implications). The next step is to compose a topic sentence for each of those themes: a specific, clear, supportable claim about what the data indicate.

We recommend going from there (composing topic sentences on a few clear themes) to organizing data around each of those topic sentences—perhaps by creating an outline or flow chart. Structure the outline by those topic sentences rather than by each piece of data. This is important: the data do not organize themselves. You as the researcher are the agent. You decide the ordering of points, and you plug in the data as evidence for those points. We have seen it go the wrong way too many times: the surveys say *a*, the primary sources say *b* and *c*, and many of the secondary sources seem to corroborate the survey respondents (*a*), but a few others say something entirely different (*d* and *e*). When research reports are organized by the data they are messy and confusing, whipping around from one piece of evidence to the next without a sense of control or clear meaning. Successful researchers analyze the data first to identify the implications/themes. The implications of the research are the most interesting points. Then researchers figure out which pieces of data support each of those implications. The difference is enormous between listing a bunch of data that needs to be made sense of and stating clear, focused claims backed up by data.

The data may be represented as evidence in many different forms, including textual evidence (quotations and paraphrases); quotations from survey responses, interviews, or focus groups; and/or tables or graphs of quantitative data. However the data are represented, remember that they play a supporting role. They are the back-up to the claims you make.

Analyzing quantitative data

A full explanation of how to analyze quantitative data is beyond the scope of this book. Students who have taken a course in quantitative research methods may be able to conduct a *multivariate analysis* of their data, which involves the examination of multiple variables in the data in relationship to one another (e.g., correlations among 300 college-student participants' ages, genders, years of dancing, and number of minutes spent practicing dance per week). However, that level of analysis requires statistical calculation skills that are not typically expected in the field of dance. This discussion sticks to the terms and types of calculations involved in *univariate* (single variable) and *bivariate* (two variables in interaction with each other) quantitative analysis.

If your research involves a quantitative survey, questionnaire, and/or tests, you have an array of software platforms for building the research instrument, distributing it, collecting data, and even doing preliminary analysis. Platforms such as Survey Monkey, Wufoo, and Qualtrics generate reports and allow users to download data into Excel to create customized spreadsheets and conduct analysis. While those user-friendly ways of reporting data help even those without statistical training to capture and compare data, the researcher's own analysis is needed to explain the relationships within and significance of the information. The following explanations are intended to guide that analysis with regard to fundamental quantitative data. The terms used here apply to most types of quantitative data, including those discussed in Chapter 5: surveys/questionnaires, pre and posttests, structural analysis, and statistical analysis.

Correlation

Correlation is the relationship between two or more data points, such that when one piece of data changes for a certain sample of the population, the other changes too—either in the same or the opposite direction. For example, there is a statistical correlation, or relationship, between the highest level of education a group of people have completed and their income levels. There is also a correlation/relationship (though in the opposite direction) between a population's highest level of education completed and their rates of cigarette smoking. Correlation is not the same as *causation*. Correlation indicates that a relationship exists but does not on its own show that one thing caused the other.

Direct correlation/positive correlation/direct relationship

These three interchangeable terms all refer to a "positive" relationship between two or more data points. A positive relationship means that when one data point increases, the other does too; when one decreases, so does the other. For example, a population's highest level of education completed and their income levels have a positive correlation or direct relationship, according to many studies. When one is high, the other tends to be too; when one is low, the other usually is as well.

Inverse correlation/negative correlation/inverse relationship

These interchangeable terms all indicate an inverse or negative correlation between two more data points; the data points go in opposite directions when there is a negative correlation. When one increases, the other tends to decrease, and vice versa. Using the same example set above, one would see in many studies that highest education completed tends to have an inverse relationship with rates of cigarette smoking. In other words, the more education a person completes, the less likely that person is to smoke cigarettes on a regular basis. The negative correlation occurs the opposite way too: someone who smokes cigarettes frequently is less likely to have completed college.

Frequency distribution

A frequency distribution is a display of how often (how frequently) members of a particular population sample gave particular responses (or did particular behaviors or said particular words). A frequency distribution table shows how many participants gave each response (on a survey or test question) or how many times a phenomenon occurred (in a structural analysis).

For the purposes of defining some key terms, consider a survey of 300 dance students that includes the question, *How many years have you been dancing?* The multiple-choice options are: (a) less than two years; (b) two to three years; (c) four to six years; (d) seven to ten years; and (e) ten years or more. Table 6.1 outlines the responses based on gender identity.

Table 6.2 shows the *frequency distribution* by gender of the particular response (e) ten years or more. The frequency distribution of male students who reported dancing for ten years or more is 35. These data could be used for a bivariate analysis of gender identity correlated with years of dancing.

Basic statistical terms

- *Mean*: average of all the scores (Using the mean has drawbacks when there are extreme or outlier scores, which skew the mean.)
- *Median*: the middle score when all responses are ranked
- *Mode*: the most frequently occurring score or phenomenon
- *Range*: the difference between the highest and lowest responses.
- *Standard deviation*: how much participants' scores differ from the mean (average) score (i.e., the deviation of each score from the mean/average)

TABLE 6.1 Length of time dancing, by gender identity

Gender identity	< 2 years	2–3 years	4–6 years	7–10 years	> 10 years	Total
Female	11	17	29	43	82	182
Male	8	18	14	30	35	105
Other or prefer not to answer	2	0	5	2	4	13
Total	21	35	48	75	121	300

TABLE 6.2 Ten years or more of dancing, by gender identity

Gender identity	Frequency	%
Female	82	68%
Male	35	29%
Other or prefer not to answer	4	3%
Total	121	100%

Structural analysis in dance

An example of a quantitative structural analysis in dance is a study of two famous choreographers' dance notations of the same ballet, choreographed 50 years apart. Several notations for dance movements from each choreographer at the same point in the music were lined up next to each other and displayed in a comprehensive table of notations so that the reader could easily note the biggest differences. The undergraduate researcher compared the notations and analyzed why the choreographers might have chosen particular movements at particular points in the music. The quantitative data (notation comparisons) were not meaningful on their own. It was the student's analysis of the choreographers' choices that illuminated the information and allowed him to put forth an interesting set of conclusions about the decisions of different choreographers when composing ballet for the same piece of music.

Analyzing qualitative data

The metaphor of unpacking luggage is an apt description of how to analyze qualitative data, including primary and secondary source texts, research-journal notes, participant responses (from open-response survey questions, interviews, or focus groups), and any other information that cannot be quantified. Imagine taking each piece of qualitative data, one by one, out of its place and holding it up for examination. What is interesting about it? How is it different from the other things (the other data points) right next to it? With what else does it logically go? Asking and answering those kinds of questions about qualitative data help bring the information to life, in a way. Thinking about the interesting qualities of each piece of data helps you to put together a meaningful story from your own interpretation of the data.

Coding

An example of qualitative data analysis comes from a student who conducted focus groups with undergraduate dance majors who participated in an after-school dance program for elementary students in an underserved school. The student-researcher asked open-ended questions about the efficacy of the program and its potential benefits for both mentors and mentees, recorded the responses, and transcribed them. The student's transcription of the responses was only the first step of data analysis. Next, she examined the transcript for patterns. Every time the idea of "giving back" or "paying forward" came up in the participants' responses, she highlighted the text in yellow. When participants described positive relationships with their mentees, the comments were highlighted in blue. Comments about the mentors improving their own dance practice as a result of their mentoring work were highlighted in green. Indications of frustration with the mentees' lack of commitment were highlighted in pink, etc. Then, examining a multi-colored transcript of the focus group discussion, the student-researcher could identify some prominent themes—namely that the mentors mentioned rewards nearly three times as often as frustrations or difficulties, and that the most frequently mentioned rewards were a sense of satisfaction in giving back to the community and appreciation for their relationships with mentees.

That form of qualitative data analysis is known as *coding*. Similar data—or pieces of data that share the same idea—are coded by theme. The coding can be done by hand on hard copies using colored highlighters or annotations by pen or pencil (e.g., asterisk as one code, check-mark as another, etc.), or on computer using the highlighter function in word-processing programs. For large data sets, coding can be done using analytical software (e.g., SPSS, Nvivo, Dedoose) that organizes pieces of text by code/theme.

Limitations of the research

As explained in Chapter 5, every research study has certain limitations. Every researcher is limited by time, resources, access to information, etc. When the limitations of the study significantly affect results, researchers need to identify the issue and explain the ramifications. What if, for example, a student studying a lesser-known but important choreographer discovered in the course of the research that primary sources and other archival materials about the choreographer were less informative than the student first thought they would be? Not all would be lost, especially if some recordings of the choreographer's dances were available for analysis; but the influences from the choreographer's personal relationships, thought to factor into her work, could not be fairly determined from the few journal entries and letters that survive. That lack of information and its impact on the research should be noted and discussed.

Questions for discussion

1. Are you most drawn to qualitative or quantitative analysis?
2. What about mixed-methods research?
3. What happens when the results are not what you expected?

Reference

analysis. (2010). In *Online Etymology Dictionary*. Retrieved from http://www.etymonline. com/index.php?allowed_in_frame=0&search=analysis

7

ARTS-BASED RESEARCH IN DANCE

Ann-Thomas Moffett

Summary

This chapter provides an overview of arts-based research (ABR), an innovative approach to scholarly work that breaks out of the quantitative versus qualitative research paradigm by using the practice and performance of the arts as a vehicle for exploring complex research topics. For dance students, ABR has the potential to bridge areas of learning within a student's dance education, including choreography, performance, and research. It can also help students apply dance knowledge and skills to research questions beyond the field of dance. This chapter discusses strategies for utilizing dance choreography and improvisation within the analysis phase of the research design. Potential research topics, sample abstracts, and links to dances created using ABR methods are included. See Figure 7.1.

What is ABR?

ABR is a ground-breaking paradigm of scholarly inquiry that emerged from, but is distinct from, qualitative research. It is based in the notion that practicing and performing in the arts can lead to discovery and creation of new knowledge. Arts-based researchers acknowledge the synergy of artistic creation and scholarly research as being centered in critical and creative inquiry. In ABR projects, artists may serve as researchers themselves or may work in a collaborative relationship with the researchers. Initially, ABR was seen as a subset of methodological tools within the qualitative research paradigm, but the field is evolving quickly and today ABR scholars position it as a distinct research paradigm that uses the arts in one or more phases of the research design (Leavy, 2015). ABR scholar Shaun McNiff (2008) defines ABR as the "systematic use of the artistic process, the

FIGURE 7.1 *The power of walking together* (Moffett, 2016)
Choreography: A. T. Moffett. Photo credit: Dan Dunlap.

actual making of artistic expressions as a primary way of understanding and examining experience by both the researchers and the people they involve in their studies" (McNiff, 2008, p. 29).

Dance-specific ABR

ABR has the potential to engage aesthetics, form and technique, and real world social content (Norris, 2011; Barone & Eisner, 2012). Dance-based methods of choreography and improvisation may be partnered with complementary qualitative methods such as interviews and focus groups, to study a research topic. Choreography may be used in the analysis phase as a component of the data triangulation process (see Chapter 6). ABR can also investigate the choreographic processes itself. Dance-specific ABR aligns with phenomenological and postmodernist inquiry, in that it seeks to investigate, describe, and deepen understanding of the lived-body experience of a phenomena. Dance arts-based researchers position "the body as a place of knowing" (Snowber, 2018, p. 247). Dancers can use their skills in physical thinking (McGregor, 2012), embodiment, and expression to support their scholarly inquiries.

Dancers, particularly modern dancers, have a long history of using choreography to challenge societal norms, to ask questions through the body and to
"externalize authentic, personal experience" (John Martin, cited in Cohen,
1966, p. 4). ABR is relevant for undergraduate dance students who are developing their theoretical knowledge and practical skills in dance. ABR enables
dancers to build bridges across the different domains of dance creative practice:
research, choreography, teaching, and performance and, therefore, to experience a holistic approach to their dance education where theory and practice
run parallel (Wilson & Moffett, 2017). Perhaps even more importantly, ABR
has the potential to help students connect their dance education to the larger
world and the complex questions that are important to them.

In the field of dance, forerunners to ABR include artist scholars such as
Katherine Dunham and Pearl Primus. In the 1940s, these two women conducted anthropological fieldwork and used dance as a lens through which to
study cultures in the Caribbean and West Africa. Dunham used a "research-
to-performance methodology" (Roberts, 2014) to transform her scholarship
into theatrical performances presented in the United States that educated
audiences about Black cultural experiences and heritage and challenged racial
segregation.

Data analysis through dance

Dance practices in choreography and improvisation may be used in the analysis
phase of research. In Katherine Boydell's qualitative study (2011) on barriers to
care for youth experiencing psychosis, she partnered with a choreographer and
dance company to analyze the data collected by the research team in the form of
case studies, field notes, and interviews. The choreographer and her company
used this data to create the research-based choreographic work "Hearing Voices."
The collaborative partnership not only helped to shape the research findings into
an accessible performance format, but it also allowed the existing data to be
explored symbolically and phenomenologically using the dance elements of
space, time, and energy. Thus, using choreographic tools, researchers accessed
additional perspectives of data from the reinterpretation of the data from the
artists (Boydell, 2011).

Dance methods used in ABR are the same ones students are already exploring in
their studio dance courses in choreography, improvisation, and performance.
Examples include body-based practices that elicit movement, and compositional
devices used to develop movement phrases into larger works. In choreographic
work created within an ABR framework, the emergent dances are a collage of
embodied knowledge and stories held within the bodies of the dancers, crafted into
a cohesive work of art that is dually focused on aesthetics and the research question. Studio courses where movement is the primary learning modality have great
potential for integrating choreographic movement theories from the dance lineage
(s) with methods of research.

Using dance creative practices in the analysis phase often merges reflective writing and movement. In *Same Story, Different Countries (SSDC)*, an ABR project exploring the personal and societal impact of racism in the United States and South Africa, choreographers and performers worked together to analyze the data gathered through literature reviews, historians' talks, and visual art from an auto-ethnographic perspective. Bridging personal stories and experiences of racism with their historical counterpart (Wilson & Moffett, 2017) was done through reflective writing, group discussions, and the excavating movement from the stories and experiences held within the body. Dance artist and activist Lela Aisha Jones, director of the Philadelphia-based company FlyGround, describes the process as "mining, witnessing, and archiving." Dancers mine their body to uncover their own connection to the content and then express it through movement, dialogue, and journaling. They witness that process in and with their fellow dancers and then collectively archive both the movement and states of body that these processes elicit. One example from the choreographic process of *SSDC*, which was used in the analysis phase, was exploring instructions for non-violent protest from the publication *A Manual for Direct Action: Strategy and Tactics for Civil Rights and All Other Nonviolent Protest Movements* (Oppenheimer & Lakey, 1965) in a phenomenological way, using the dance elements of space, time, and energy. The text served as an impetus for creating vignettes and tableaus that embodied the actions *resist* and *carry*. This choreographic process adapted post-modern, task-based methods to enable the dancers to create relationships through movement and to design the stage space based on the simulated world created by the artists' connection to ideas in the text and the broader research topic (see Figure 7.2).

ABR is a meaningful launching point into the practice of research for under-graduate dance students because it enables an application of dance/body-based knowledge and skills that they are cultivating in their dance education. The range of potential research topics is vast. Dance-driven ABR may be an investigation into one of the domains of dance creative practice: create, perform, connect, and respond (National Core Arts Standards). It may also be an interdisciplinary topic, which merges students' dance studies with other majors, minors, or areas of interest. Suggested topics are as follows:

- Choreographic process of a guest artist
- Embodying vocabulary and style in the technique class
- Perceptions of body image by college dance students
- Ethnographic study of dance practices/culture in a study abroad experience
- Dance integration in education
- Group dynamics
- Understanding resilience in undergraduate students
- The impact of handheld technology on interpersonal relationships
- Veteran and civilian perceptions of re-entry

FIGURE 7.2 *Continuum of action the witness spectrum* (Jones, 2016)
Choreography: Lela Aisha Jones. Photo credit: Dan Dunlap.

Sample abstracts of ABR projects involving dance

Making sense of collective events: The co-creation of a research based dance

(Boydell, 2011)

Abstract: A symbolic interaction (BLUMER, 1969; MEAD, 1934; PRUS, 1996; PRUS & GRILLS, 2003) approach was taken to study the collective event (PRUS, 1997) of creating a research-based dance on pathways to care in first episode psychosis. Viewing the co-creation of a research-based dance as collective activity attends to the processual aspects of an individual's experiences. It allowed us to study the process of the creation of the dance and its capacity to convert abstract research into concrete form and to produce generalizable abstract knowledge from the empirical research findings. Thus, through the techniques of movement, metaphor, voice-over, and music, the characterization of experience through dance was personal and generic, individual and collective, particular and trans-situational. The dance performance allowed us to address the visceral, emotional, and visual aspects of our research which are frequently invisible in traditional academia.

Dance as intervention: Disrupting gender norms of embodiment

(Migdalek, 2015a)

Abstract: This article describes, and comments on, the process of using dance as an effective research tool through which to self-reflexively research one's embodied habitus. It refers to research that I conducted into notions of masculine and feminine norms of embodiment commonly prescribed as fitting for one's biological sex. This research extends to an investigation into modes of thinking and doing into which I was inducted as a male dancer and as a person in the everyday. The process of creating what was to become a danced physical theater performance piece proved to be both emotionally confronting and enlightening. It also served as a form of intervention. Not only has critical interrogation of my own practices and aesthetic sensibilities as a male dancer, choreographer, and dance educator shifted and enhanced my perspectives and understandings of gender and embodiment, but it has also disrupted embedded and habituated ways in which I operated in dance and other contexts. In addition, the performance piece, *Gender Icons*, has generated profound responses in a number of my fieldwork participants, indicating that dance research also has the capacity for raising social consciousness in others.

Building bridges for dance through arts-based research

(Wilson & Moffett, 2017)

Abstract: This paper considers arts-based research (ABR) as a useful resource for creating fluid and dialogic spaces between multiple domains of dance knowledge and practices. Through the lens of a multi-disciplinary, arts-based research project *Same Story, Different Countries* explored the socio-political phenomena of racism in the United States and South Africa. The paper illuminates how arts-based research can bridge important areas of learning, in particular artistic knowledge and social justice learning for postsecondary dance students, teachers and artists. Using a mixed method of qualitative techniques and artistic dance practices the study captured and analyzed dance participants' perspectives on the benefits of being involved in the project. The project was found to increase participants' knowledge of various dance practices (performance, choreography, teaching, research) while simultaneously deepening their understanding of racism and racial injustice, and awakening their sense of social responsibility. Three major themes emerged from the findings: connectedness, transformation and empowerment toward action in future dance practices. In empowering the dance participants, and creating bridges for them between dance and its multiple domains, and dance and the larger social world, this paper advocates that arts-based research is valuable to the future growth and relevance of postsecondary dance education.

Modeling innovative methodological practices in a dance/family studies transdisciplinary project

(Sharp & DeCesaro, 2015)

Abstract: Using our dance/family studies transdisciplinary project as a site of analysis, we review the existing literature of arts/social science endeavors and share innovative methodological practices from our project. Unlike most arts/social science endeavors, our project is transdisciplinary and is based on a collaboration between a trained choreographer and dancer and a trained family scholar. The transdisciplinary nature of our project is highlighted in the choreographer's kinesthetic analysis of the family scholar's qualitative data, the use of a pilot study, duo-memoing, and a strong commitment to sharing authorship of all our writing. Throughout the article, we highlight the benefits of our work for the field of family studies.

Bodily writing and performative inquiry: Inviting an arts-based research methodology into collaborative doctoral research vocabularies

(Buono & Gonzalez, 2017)

Abstract: In this article, the authors (then two doctoral students) describe their methodology of engaging in an interdisciplinary, collaborative doctoral arts-based research (ABR) project. Education and the arts were integrated utilizing dance methods of bodily writing and performative inquiry to strengthen the analysis of dissertation findings in the field of teacher education. We share our theoretical stance based on somatics, embodiment, and rhizomatics, followed by a thick description of our rhizomatic actions of becoming collaborative arts-based researchers. We advocate, argue, and fight for the right to introduce and encourage interdisciplinary and collaborative research with the arts in doctoral students' studies and highlight the implications our project had on accessibility to research and engagement with broader audiences as well as our entrant-audience. We argue that ultimately, combining efforts to bring collaborative interdisciplinary ABR into doctoral students' work will foster benefits for both doctoral students and the research produced.

Sample of dances created through ABR methods

Embodied iconics of gender

(Migdalek, 2015b)

Choreography by Jack Migdalek, https://vimeo.com/115959772

The power of walking together, in Same story, different countries

(Moffett, 2016)

Choreography by A. T. Moffett, https://vimeo.com/175884381

Trois chaises en la paix et en la guerre, deux libraires, la feminine and le masculine, l'enseignenment de Rancierre?

(Blumenfeld-Jones, 2017)

Choreography by Donald Blumenfeld-Jones, https://www.youtube.com/watch?v=aStFZpijwno

The zen of laundry

(Snowber, 2010)

Choreography by Celeste Snowber, https://www.youtube.com/watch?v=j7kz8yyzrCM

Discussion questions

1. In an ABR project, how many stages should utilize artistic tools?
2. How can ABR benefit undergraduate dance students?
3. What challenges do you anticipate when engaging in ABR projects?
4. How is choreography similar to research?
5. Name a potential ABR research topic that combines your dance studies with an additional major or minor.
6. What improvisational scores from dance composition might be useful in analyzing data through movement?
7. How might reflective writing in dance technique class contribute to an ABR project?

References

Barone, T., & Eisner, E. (2012). *Arts-based research.* Thousand Oaks, CA: SAGE Publications Inc.

Blumenfeld-Jones, D. (2017). Trois chaises en la paix et en la guerre, deux libraires, la feminine and le masculine, l'enseignenment de Rancierre? Retrieved from https://www.youtube.com/watch?v=aStFZpijwno

Boydell, K. (2011). Making sense of collective events: The co-creation of a research based dance. *Forum: Qualitative Social Research*, 12(1). Retrieved from http://dx.doi.org/10.17169/fqs-12.1.1525

Buono, A., & Gonzalez, H. C. (2017). Bodily writing and performative inquiry: Inviting an arts-based research methodology into collaborative doctoral research vocabularies. *International Journal of Education & the Arts*, 18(36). Retrieved from http://www.ijea.org/v18n36/

Cohen, S. J. (1966). Introduction: The caterpillar's question. In S. J. Cohen (Ed.), *The modern dance: Seven statements of belief*. Middletown, CT: Wesleyan University Press.

Jones, L. (2016). Continuum of action the witness spectrum. "Same Story" Different Countries. Baby Grand Theatre, Wilmington, DE.

Leavy, P. (2015). *Method meets art: Arts-based research practice*. 2nd ed. New York City: The Guilford Press.

McGregor, W. (2012). A choreographer's creative process in real time. TED Ideas Worth Spreading. Retrieved from https://www.ted.com/talks/wayne_mcgregor_a_choreographer_s_creative_process_in_real_time

McNiff, S. (2008). Arts based research. In J. Knowles, & A. Cole (Eds.), *Handbook of the arts in qualitative research: Perspectives, methodologies, examples, and issues* (pp. 29–41). Thousand Oaks, CA: SAGE Publications, Inc.

Migdalek, J. (2015a). Dance as intervention: Disrupting gender norms of embodiment. *Critical approaches to arts-based research: UNESCO observatory multi-disciplinary journal in the arts*, 1(5). Retrieved from https://education.unimelb.edu.au/__data/assets/pdf_file/0005/2630966/UNESCO-E-JOURNAL-V5I1-02-MIGDALEK.pdf

Migdalek, J. (2015b). Embodied iconics of gender. Retrieved from https://vimeo.com/115959772

Moffett, A. T. (2016). Power of walking together. *"Same Story" Different Countries*. Baby Grand Theatre, Wilmington, DE.

Norris, J. (2011). Towards the use of the 'great wheel' as a model in determining the quality and merit of arts-based projects (research and instruction). *International Journal of Education & the Arts*, 12(SI 1.7), 1–24. Retrieved from https://eric.ed.gov/?id=EJ937078

Oppenheimer, M., & Lakey, G.(1965). *A manual for direct action: Strategy and tactics for civil rights and all other nonviolent protest movements*. Chicago:Quadrangle Books, Inc.

Roberts, R. (2014). Research-performance methodology: Embodying knowledge and power from the field to the concert stage. In E. Chin (Ed.), *Katherine Dunham: Recovering an anthropological legacy, choreographing ethnographic futures* (pp. 17–30). Santa Fe, NM: School for Advanced Research Press.

Sharp, E. A., & Durham DeCesaro, G. (2015). Modeling innovative methodological practices in a dance/family studies transdisciplinary project. *Journal of Family Theory & Review*, 7(4), 367–380. Retrieved from https://onlinelibrary.wiley.com/doi/pdf/10.1111/jftr.12109

Snowber, C. (2010). The zen of laundry. Retrieved from https://www.youtube.com/watch?v=j7kz8yyzrCM

Snowber, C. (2018). Living, moving, and dancing: Embodied ways of inquiry. In P. Leavy (Ed.), *Handbook of arts-based research* (pp. 247–266). New York, NY: The Guilford Press.

Wilson, L., & Moffett, A. T. (2017). Building bridges for dance through arts-based research. *Research in Dance Education*, 18(2), 135–149. Retrieved from https://doi.org/10.1080/14647893.2017.1330328

8

CITING SOURCES

Jenny Olin Shanahan

Summary

Responsible scholars give credit to other researchers, authors, and performers by correctly acknowledging ideas, words, images, and performances (live or via recording) that are not their own. Giving credit is accomplished through the use of citations and bibliographies. This chapter discusses Modern Language Association (MLA), Chicago (and Turabian, a variation of Chicago), American Psychological Association (APA), and Harvard citation guidelines as well as some of the reasons for using different citation and reference styles. Plagiarism encompasses a wide spectrum of behaviors, from outright word-for-word copying of another's work to artful paraphrasing that re-states another author's idea without acknowledgment. Using images and recordings that belong to others without securing permission and/or without correct attribution is also plagiarism. We provide guidelines and resources to help students navigate the challenge of properly citing others' ideas, words, images, and performances and avoiding unethical uses of information.

Rationale

Scholarly inquiry is the pursuit of knowledge and truth, so conducting research and creative scholarship honestly is fundamental to the task. Every scholar has the responsibility to demonstrate absolute integrity in the reporting of data, acknowledging the sources of ideas and information, sharing images and recordings only with permission, and providing thorough and correct documentation of those sources.

In this chapter we seek to shift some common perspectives on research integrity and the citation and documentation of sources. Many of our students have expressed a sense of fear or frustration about the topic of citations and bibliographies. They have too often been made to feel as if they could fail an assignment due to plagiarism for making an honest and fairly minor mistake in citation. At the other end of the spectrum we have had many students who assume that in a world of easy access to free information, music, and videos, there is no big deal in sharing and appropriating each other's work. Both attitudes are missing the mark and creating unnecessary problems for students, especially those involved in under-graduate research. Let us see if we can redefine the mark by clarifying a reasonable goal of honesty and integrity in scholarly work.

Plagiarism

The definition of plagiarism is taking someone else's ideas or other intellectual property (including creative work) and representing them, in whole or in part, as your own. Plagiarism is a form of theft, as the ideas and creative work of one person are taken without their consent by someone else who hopes to benefit from them. In the United States and many other countries we share a legal standard and cultural understanding that each person's ideas and creative works (which are usually repre-sented in the products of the ideas, such as works of art, recordings, and pieces of writing) are uniquely their own. When the ideas are shared—whether in the form of a film, blog post, song, essay, presentation, performance, etc.—the creator/writer enters into an implicit trust with those who encounter it. The original creator/writer trusts that shared values and legal standards will keep his/her own name and rights attached to it—that anyone else who shares or builds upon the work will give the creator the credit that is due and, in terms of creative work, share it only with permission.

Guidelines for attributions and citations

Students and other scholars who incorporate others' ideas, words, images, and recordings into their own are required to identify clearly the original sources of the ideas, no matter how easily accessible the information may be. Work found on online platforms such as Creative Commons that allow creators to share licensed and copyrighted works for others to use legally needs to be cited as well. The Creative Commons website has clear examples of how to attribute and cite different kinds of media, depending on the terms of use. The guidance Creative Commons provides is to use the acronym TASL to remember to attribute and cite the Title, Author, Source, and License, as Creative Commons offers six types of licenses that determine how material can be used and shared, and each work on the platform includes information about its particular license (Creative Commons, 2018).

Videos also must be attributed and cited, even when they are readily available on YouTube or other free sites. For purposes of attribution and citation, the name of the person who posted the video is treated as the "author"; that individual's screen name (username in YouTube) should be cited for retrievability, along with their real name, if known. When you know the person's real name and screen name, the real name is what appears in parenthetical citations; both appear on the bibliography, with the real name listed first. Live performances are cited with as much of the following information as is available: the title of the performance (which is listed first in Chicago, Turabian and APA style bibliographies); name of the choreographer, director, and/or creator (which is listed first in MLA style bibliographies); key performers' names; venue, city, and state; and date of the performance.

Even those not intending to steal or cause harm may be committing ethics violations that have consequences, so it is incumbent on researchers to document all sources of information, images, and recordings. When they intend to give credit but make an omission or other mistake, students may be more guilty of sloppy scholarship than outright plagiarism. While it may not be an illegal offense, sloppy scholarship should be guarded against by taking care in the work and double-checking that all sources of information are correctly credited.

The intentional appropriation of others' ideas without giving credit is much more serious, of course. University policies and academic publishers dictate serious consequences for those who are caught plagiarizing or committing other violations in research ethics. Strict policies and severe consequences are intended to discourage such violations, for if plagiarism occurs without significant repercussions, everyone's work is diminished. For that reason, plagiarism can ruin a scholar's career. Other ethical and legal violations include fabricating or falsifying data and improperly treating human subjects/participants (including any violation of IRB guidelines).

Why there are different citation and documentation styles

In our various academic disciplines we are all in agreement about the utmost importance of academic integrity and the lawful and ethical crediting of the sources of ideas. We have different guidelines for exactly how we do that crediting, though, based in our disciplinary epistemologies, or theories and ways of knowing (see Chapter 5). When students are required to use MLA format in their first-year writing course and, just when they have that down, are expected to switch to the APA style in their education or other social science classes—and then Chicago, Turabian, or Harvard style in their dance courses, they may be understandably frustrated. We have heard more than once students bemoaning different citation styles as a conspiracy to drive them mad.

Believe it or not, however, there are some sound reasons for the different expectations. We have found that understanding the epistemologies and underlying reasons for different citation and bibliographic styles helps ease the frustration. Graff and Birkenstein's (2014) *"They Say, I Say": The Moves that Matter in Academic Writing* very helpfully addresses the concept of templates in academic writing. Graff and Birkenstein point out that many of our disciplinary conventions follow certain patterns or templates, and that by learning some of the main ones we can master aspects of academic writing with more alacrity.

Our colleague Herb Childress (2017) applies the idea of templates to understanding different citation systems and the disciplinary values they represent. Dr.

Childress uses examples of MLA and APA parenthetical citations and bibliographic entries to make the point. MLA parenthetical citations require the author's last name and the page number on which the idea is stated. In APA format the parenthetical citation includes the author's last name and year of publication. The only time the page number is provided is when the text is quoted directly, which is rare in APA papers. Why the differences? MLA is the format used in the humanities, disciplines in which elegant writing and textual analysis are highly valued. Humanities scholars need the page number or URL in the parenthetical citation because reading the actual words of the text is usually important to them. APA, however, is used most often in social sciences, where different primary values are in play: timeliness—hence the use of the year of publication in the parenthetical citation—and the empirical/experimental findings themselves, as opposed to the prose in which they were reported. That is why APA papers include few if any direct quotations: the findings are what matter, not the way in which the researchers expressed them, so paraphrases do not lose the essence of the ideas.

The bibliographic entries of each style likewise reflect disciplinary priorities. On an MLA Works Cited page, authors' first and last names are listed, whereas APA uses last name only and initials. Why? The fullness of the human person is not only a subject of study but a deeply held value in the humanities. A scholar's full name conveys more about that person than his or her initials, including in many cases his or her gender identity. The scientific approach favored in disciplines that use APA style has a preference for more neutrality. There is no way to know the gender identity of a scholar from first and middle initials alone, and that is considered a good thing in objective research. Another notable difference between the two bibliographic styles is the placement of the year of publication: near the end of the entry in MLA Works Cited, but right after the authors' names—second thing in the entry—in APA References. The privileging of timely research is again the reason for the early placement of the date in APA References entries. In the humanities, however, timeliness may not matter at all. For people who study ancient and classical texts, there is timelessness in human wisdom. The year of publication is one of the least important pieces of information, so it is relegated to the end of the entry.

Childress's (2017) ideas can be extended to Chicago and Turabian styles, used most often in history and the fine arts, including dance. As with MLA, Chicago and Turabian styles include authors' full names (not just initials for first and middle names) in the bibliography. But as with APA, Chicago and Turabian styles require the year of publication in parenthetical citations and in a location closer to the beginning of each entry in bibliographies. Perhaps it is no surprise that scholars in the field of dance most often use Chicago citation style, as it reflects values of timeliness of research as well as of the fuller identity of authors and artists.

The last citation and reference style we will mention, Harvard style, is similar to APA, with small differences with regard to where parentheses go. According to the Harvard College Library (2017), the Harvard citation style was named for the Harvard faculty who first used it in the late 19th century. Although the style's name is connected to the first institution of higher education in the United States, Harvard citations are mainly used now in the United Kingdom and Australia.

Online quick guides for citation and referencing, including OWL at Purdue

Even though we can understand some of the reasons for different citation and bibliographic styles, it is difficult to master and remember them. And even when we do master one or two styles with which we work most regularly, a new edition of the style book is published, and we have some new details to try to keep in mind. Fortunately, holding all of that in one's own mind is not necessary beyond the basics, and keeping up with the changes can be fairly automatic.

We urge caution in using "easy" citation and bibliography generators because they do not always align accurately with the style guides' organizations, especially because of the wide array of types of texts and media being used by scholars today. Checking those sites against the latest style guides is a good idea. We recommend that instead of relying on automatic but sometimes inaccurate bibliography generations you create your own citations and bibliographies by following the templates for your preferred style guide, most of which are free and accessible online. The Online Writing Lab (OWL) at Purdue University is an outstanding resource for APA and MLA. It comprises examples of citations and bibliographic entries for a wide variety of sources. If you use APA or MLA, we recommend bookmarking the website (http s://owl.english.purdue.edu/owl/) and keeping it open while writing. Through a quick search and a look at some examples from a reputable source, anyone can be sure of correct, up-to-date citing and referencing.

Questions for discussion

1. What are the consequences for plagiarism in undergraduate research?
2. What if I didn't mean to plagiarize?
3. How do I cite things that are not written texts, such as photos and videos?

References

Childress, H. (2017). Templates: XS/S/M/L. Workshop presented at the Council on Undergraduate Research Institute: Undergraduate Research and Creative Inquiry in the Arts and Humanities, Lincoln University, PA.

Creative Commons. (2018). How to give attribution. Retrieved from https://creativecomm ons.org/use-remix/get-permission/

Graff, G., & Birkenstein, C. (2014). *"They say, I say": The moves that matter in academic writing.* New York: W. W. Norton.

Harvard College Library. (2017). What is the Harvard system for citing references? Retrieved from https://ask.library.harvard.edu/faq/81735

9

DISSEMINATION OF RESULTS

Jenny Olin Shanahan

Summary

Included in the Council on Undergraduate Research (CUR) definition of undergraduate research (UR) is the phrase "contribution to the discipline." As with faculty scholarship, UR and creative inquiry contribute to the discipline through dissemination of the work to other scholars, in the form of publications, conference presentations, performances, and exhibits. There is a growing number of opportunities for students to perform, present, publish, and show their work, and this chapter provides a guide for students and faculty alike as to the various venues, conferences, symposia, and journals available to students.

Why share your work?

The key attribute that transforms ordinary students doing research assignments into *scholars* is the dissemination of their results. Scholars are part of a *scholarly community* that learns from each other and advances the field of study or another form of community. That learning from each other can only occur, of course, when scholars share what they learn, discover, or create. One purpose of conducting research and creative inquiry is to inform one's own thinking. But the more important reason is to contribute to the discovery and creation of new knowledge and new artistic expression. In sharing new knowledge and artistic creations, scholars further not only their own, but also many others' understanding about the topic of study and contribute to the progression of the field.

Dissemination as a defining feature of UR

The definition of "undergraduate research" according to the national organization CUR is "a faculty-mentored inquiry or investigation conducted by a student that *makes an original intellectual or creative contribution to the discipline*" (Council on Under-graduate Research, 2011; emphasis added). The mentored inquiry or investigation would be incomplete without the *contribution* (through dissemination) to the discipline, or to another community as appropriate. That "original … contribution to the discipline" is a very high standard; any scholar's work could shoot for that goal and not always get there, for any number of reasons. It could turn out that another scholar made the discovery first. Sometimes limitations of studies (see Chapter 5) are more significant than initially realized and then undermine the results. Or, even after a thoughtfully chosen design, a study may not go as planned, and the data could be inconclusive. Achieving publishable results that make a notable disciplinary contribution is not the only standard for successful UR, nor is it the only reason to disseminate findings. We usually talk with our students in terms of a slightly edited version of the CUR defini-tion of UR: a faculty-mentored investigation that *seeks to make* an original intellectual or creative contribution. *Seeking to make* a contribution puts the focus on the process and purpose of conducting scholarly work. It does not depend on an entirely successful contribution. Having an orientation for your research and creative efforts toward a community of disciplinary experts, peers, and/or practitioners (e.g., dancers, choreo-graphers, teachers, and therapists) makes your work more meaningful and scholarly than if you were gathering information solely for your own knowledge base.

We have found it even more useful to identify what makes UR a "high-impact practice" (Association of American Colleges & Universities, 2015—the characteristics or criteria of impactful scholarly experiences, rather than a one-size-fits-all definition. Osborn and Karukstis (2009) laid out four criteria of high-quality UR: mentorship by faculty, original work, acceptability in the discipline, and dissemination. In this chapter we are most interested in that last criterion, dissemination. Dissemination is considered a defining characteristic of UR because sharing the results of scholarly work with an audience of academics, peers, experts in the field, a community of practice (a group of people who share a common interest and wish to learn from each other about it), and/or the general public, completes the inquiry process and is a powerful learning experience in its own right.

Engaging with an authentic audience

Have you ever wondered about the point of writing a research paper that only your instructor would ever read—and perhaps only cursorily, along with dozens of other students' assignments? We remember feeling let down at times during our student years, after investing late-night hours and some pretty good ideas in writing an essay, only to send it into the apparent void of a professor's paper pile. Our best professors wrote thoughtful responses to each student's work, and a couple of them even talked with us about it, but those were few and far between.

On the other hand, when students have the chance to engage with an authentic audience for their work beyond a single instructor, they say they devote more time and effort to it. As university faculty we have witnessed the difference in the quality of student work when it will be disseminated in some way. The research and writing simply matter more when other people will read or watch the results of the work and respond to it. As social creatures perhaps all of us are hard-wired to want to connect with others through our ideas and efforts. When others find our work thought-provoking, when they ask questions about it, and/or when they offer productive feedback, we tend to want to meet their expectations for good-quality work. For all of these reasons—the contributions that can be made to a scholarly community and field of study, the logical completion of the research process, and the higher level of effort and engagement inspired by addressing an audience—sharing the work is an essential aspect of UR.

What you will gain from presenting and publishing your scholarly work

You may have heard the worrisome news of the last several years that the unemployment rate for recent college graduates in the United States is well above the national average—and is even above the unemployment rate for those over age 25 *without a college degree* (National Center for Education Statistics, 2017). Underemployment—which is defined as part-time employment for those who want to work full-time and/or employment in low-skilled jobs for people with college degrees—for college graduates under age 27 is even higher: over 40% in the United States. Meanwhile, student-loan debt is at its highest point in history (National Center for Education Statistics, 2017). We share these statistics not at all to discourage you, but to make the case for doing everything you can during your undergraduate years to distinguish yourself in an intensely competitive job market and graduate-school environment.

The problem of the persistently high unemployment and underemployment rates for recent college graduates appears to be based at least in part in employers' beliefs that millennials are unprepared for skilled work. A major survey of business and nonprofit leaders commissioned by the Association of American Colleges & Universities (AAC&U) found that employers see recent college graduates as ill-prepared for career success (Hart Research Associates, 2015). Employers gave low grades to recent college graduates on all of AAC&U's learning outcomes of a college education, including six skills deemed most important for career success across a range of nonprofit and for-profit industries: (1) oral communication; (2) working effectively on teams; (3) written communication; (4) ethical decision-making; (5) critical thinking and analysis; and (6) applying knowledge to real-world problems.

Oral communication skills

Implications of the research are that students who develop particularly valued skills are likely to stand out in a very tough employment environment. Nearly all business and nonprofit leaders surveyed said those six skills are more important than a job candidate's major or the university he or she attended (Hart Research Associates, 2015). In other words, students should be focused more on oral and written communication and critical, real-world problem-solving skills than worrying about the most marketable majors or the prominence of their university. All of the skills most valued by employers are developed exceptionally well through UR. And the top-ranked skill, oral communication, is principally cultivated through presenting scholarly work. Speaking articulately and confidently and engaging interpersonally with a diversity of people are oral-communication skills that need extensive practice to develop.

It would not be at all surprising if you were reluctant (or even deathly afraid) to develop oral-communication skills by giving research presentations. Just about everyone experiences nervousness about public speaking, and for many the very idea brings on acute anxiety. According to the Chapman University Survey of American Fears, glossophobia—also known as stage fright or fear of public speaking—is one of the most common forms of personal anxiety. Fortunately, there is a plethora of online and print resources to help manage anxiety about public speaking. More severe phobia can be eased through therapy, relaxation techniques, or hypnosis.

The best strategy of all for overcoming a fear of presenting is to practice over and over again, preferably in low-stakes settings. Take opportunities to present in less stressful situations, such as in a class with people you know and can trust to be on your side, or in a student research symposium on your campus, where dozens or even hundreds of your peers are going through the same experience along with you. Public speaking is truly something that gets easier by doing it. We recommend starting out with poster presentations, if feasible. Our students have found it much less nerve-racking to speak for a few minutes with one or two audience members at a time than to give a more formal talk. After even one poster presentation you will likely gain confidence in your ability to present your work and may feel more ready to try an oral presentation in a friendly environment. (Preparing poster and oral presentations is addressed later in this chapter.)

Written communication skills

The other critical career skill that is enhanced by sharing your research is written communication. Writing the content of an oral or poster presentation or an artist's statement about a choreographed work, for example, is an excellent means of developing drafting and revision skills. Writing about the results of research is especially suited to common workplace writing situations, such as reports and presentation materials. Showing a willingness to revise written work has been cited by employers as a rare and valuable trait. Your work to revise presentations—especially in consolidating a large amount of information into a succinct and effective poster or talk—can be noted in cover letters and interviews to your benefit.

Publishing your UR will take that distinction in written-communication skills to a whole new level. Composing a substantial paper that will be carefully read by an audience—as opposed to the quick grasp they would get from presentation slides or a poster—requires writing acumen and a longer process of drafting and revision.

The work likely will pay off exceedingly well, though. Student papers published in Bridgewater State University's journal of UR, *The Undergraduate Review*, have been downloaded *over two million times*. Students whose work appears in the journal, which is published in print as well as electronic form, report being asked about their articles during interviews for internships, jobs, and graduate and professional school. They can include a link to their published paper in electronic applications, offering an at-the-ready writing sample that is not only well written, but also copyedited and nicely laid out by the journal editors. Since the published papers show up in online searches too, the students have discovered that when their names are Googled by potential employers or graduate admissions officers, what shows up, at or near the top of the results, is their published research. The benefits of that exposure of a student's best work are incalculable.

Where can you share your work?

The rhetorical situation

As you may have learned in an English composition course, the *audience, context*, and *purpose* of a piece of writing constitute its *rhetorical situation*, or the circumstances in which an argument is made. As with the concept of the rhetorical triangle explained in Chapter 5, the theory of the *rhetorical situation* derives from Aristotle's *Rhetoric*, an ancient Greek philosophical text about the art of effective speaking and writing. Bitzer (1968) adapted the concept for modern presenters and writers to explain how their claims are shaped by the intended audience (including readers), the context (or setting or framework in which the presenter/writer/performer is working), and its purpose. The following examples of each aspect of the rhetorical situation—audience, context, and purpose—are intended to help illustrate its function. Imagine sharing your research in a venue mainly attended by your college or university's dance and other arts professors. As experts in the field of study, the *audience* of professors would expect high-level scholarly work. You might, for example, decide to include theoretical ideas with which only people who study dance would be familiar. Alternatively, what if you were to present that same work in a talk at a multidisciplinary undergraduate conference attended by hundreds of college students majoring in a broad range of fields, many of whom have never taken a dance class? In that presentation you would either omit some of the theory or include only a few key points with clear explanations. The audience determines a great deal of which content you share and how you present it.

The *context* (circumstance, setting, or framework) is the second determining factor. The presentation to the dance faculty could occur in a departmental thesis defense, where you are expected to give a formal talk followed by questions from the faculty. Your skill in answering the questions as well as your ability to present your most important results succinctly and clearly are being evaluated for a grade, and may even determine whether you graduate with honors. That high-stakes context would undoubtedly influence your selection of information and how you prepare for the questions. If, however, instead of justifying your work at a thesis defense you were presenting in a less intense situation, both the substance and style of your presentation would be different. Consider, for example, presenting a poster at your university's annual undergraduate-research symposium that is held on campus. Members of that same departmental dance faculty might stop by your poster. Yet you would interact with them less formally, one or two at a time, rather than addressing the whole department at once. What you say to them would probably vary, based on how well you know each professor and how acquainted each is with your work. The context shapes the content, format, and design of the presentation.

The *purpose* of sharing the work also affects its substance and form. If you received a UR grant from the department to support your work, you would likely need to report to faculty on the selection committee about what you accomplished at the end of the grant period. Such a report could include major findings, challenges you encountered and how you addressed them, and a statement of gratitude for the opportunities afforded by the funding. But what if the grant were renewable and you wanted to request additional funds? You would still show what you accomplished with the first grant, but you would need to add a convincing explanation of how much further you would like to take the project and how a second round of funding would make that possible. In that grant-renewal request you would have a distinctly different purpose (asking for more money) and therefore would need to alter your report to achieve the hoped-for outcome. Each purpose has its own demands, and meeting those particular demands is essential to success.

This section is titled "Where can you share your work?" The answer to that question is contingent on the rhetorical situation, or the network of audience, context, and purpose. The main options are to create a performance, if you are a choreographer, to publish your research in an academic journal, and/or to present it at a conference, and there are multiple outlets and venues within those broad categories. The following possibilities for dissemination of UR in dance begin with the most accessible opportunities and move roughly to the most selective.

Campus symposium of UR and creative work

As the benefits of UR and creative inquiry as a high-impact practice become ever more widely recognized, most four-year colleges and universities in the United States now offer opportunities for students to share their scholarly work in a campus symposium or showcase of undergraduate work, most often held at the end of the academic year. Some of those events feature poster presentations exclusively, while others include a mix of poster and oral presentations and, in some cases, art displays and music, dance, and theatre performances. The size and atmosphere of campus symposia vary a great deal too. On some campuses student-presenters are selected through a review process, whereas at other institutions everyone who wants to present or perform is welcome, and many faculty even make a symposium presentation or performance a course requirement, especially for capstones and other research-intensive courses. Awards for the highest quality projects are given at many campus symposiums.

Presenting or performing in a campus symposium or showcase is an outstanding opportunity for several reasons. The symposium audience—other students, faculty and administrators, and some presenters' family members—offers a valuable and gratifying experience in addressing a real-world audience. Over the years we have each witnessed hundreds of students heading to their campus-symposium presentations with apprehension or dread, only to hear them say immediately afterward that it was not nearly as intimidating as they had feared. Many of our students have even reported that the experience was fun! One of the most satisfying professional experiences for each of us is that first conversation with a student after a presentation or performance. Students express relief that they overcame nervousness to give a solid presentation and, most exciting, gratitude for the experience of sharing their work with people genuinely interested in it. It has been through positive experiences at campus symposia that most of our students who have gone on to present and perform at national conferences gained the confidence to do so.

We encourage you to present your work in whatever venue is available on your campus, whether a showcase of work from your department or school, or a university-wide event. The practice is invaluable, and each presentation is a legitimate point of distinction on your résumé, especially with oral-communication skills so highly valued. If your college or university does not yet hold a symposium of student scholarship, you have a few options to pursue. The first is, with the support of faculty who know the quality of your work, you and some peers could request an opportunity in the department to share your work in performances, lecture-recitals, panel presentations, or even posters. Many universities' larger events started with individual department efforts. And plenty of individual departments find that they value the small seminar-style symposia so much that they will keep hosting those events even if a larger showcase takes off on their campus. The second option is to locate an institution nearby that hosts an annual symposium of student work and ask whether students from neighboring campuses could participate. Our campus symposiums welcome student-presenters from community colleges in the area. Lastly, you may find a state or regional undergraduate-research conference with the welcoming environment of a campus-based event. The large Commonwealth of Massachusetts annual conference hosted by UMass-Amherst, for example, has a high rate of acceptance and inclusive feel.

National, state, and regional undergraduate research conferences

Statewide and regional conferences of UR offer a moderate "step up" in presentation experience. Many such events accept most proposals, as they are not intended to be highly selective, but to give as many students as possible the opportunity to share their work beyond their home campuses.

The more selective state conferences are "posters at the capitol" events, for which a set number of students across that state are chosen to present posters, usually in the capitol building itself. The purposes of such events, beyond the great experience and prestige afforded the student-presenters, are to show legislators and their staff members the importance and quality of research and creative inquiry taking place in their districts and across the state, and, more or less directly, advocate for research, arts, and higher-education funding in the state. Traditionally, most of the posters at the capitol feature science, technology, engineering, and mathematics (STEM) research, but the rising recognition of the importance of scholarly work and funding for STEAM—STEM plus the arts—has brought more presentations from dance and other arts disciplines.

As faculty and administrators with long-time participation in the National Conference on Undergraduate Research (NCUR) we cannot say enough about what a valuable experience that annual event offers for student-presenters and performers. NCUR has an over-30-year tradition of bringing together thousands of students from across the nation—as well as dozens from other countries—each year on a different college campus to present their research and creative scholarship. Over 3,500 students presented at the University of Central Oklahoma in April 2018, in the form of posters, oral presentations, art exhibits with gallery talks, and lecture-recitals (in which students in the performing arts perform a piece of music or dance and provide a brief lecture on it). NCUR has a high rate of acceptances, usually over 80%, and maintains strong quality in its presentations. Besides the distinction of presenting or performing at a national conference with a large, engaged audience, NCUR offers the opportunity to meet students in your own field and every major imaginable from across the country and the world. The conference hosts a graduate-school fair of hundreds of different programs, inspiring keynote speakers, and social events. Inexpensive excursions in the local area are often available on the Saturday the conference ends, as well.

Disciplinary academic meetings/conferences

As the tide of UR has swept through higher education in the last two decades, many of the disciplinary professional organizations in which university faculty participate and present their scholarly work have provided venues for undergraduates in their respective areas to present too. Our universities' UR offices regularly receive notifications of new opportunities for students to present at academic organizations' regional and national meetings. Most of those organizations have carved out a session for undergraduates within the larger meeting, giving students the dual benefit of attending presentations by scholars in their field of study while having a space for presenting at an undergraduate level. Putting undergraduates side by side with renowned scholars can be intimidating for the students. Nonetheless, a few disciplinary conferences have gone down that route, successfully bringing together undergraduates, graduate students, and professors in shared sessions.

Opportunities in dance include the National Dance Education Organization (NDEO) national conference, which welcomes student participation, and the American College Dance Association's (ACDA) National College Dance Festival and regional festivals, which include performances based on artistic excellence, as well as workshops and intensive trainings.

UR journals

Undergraduate students who get their work published are most often published in a journal of student work. Many colleges and universities publish their own students' scholarship in a campus-based journal, in electronic and/ or print format. In addition to campus-based journals, a few college and university consortia (associations of several institutions joined by region or mission), such as the Council of Public Liberal Arts Colleges, and state-university systems publish journals featuring work by students at any of the member institutions.

A few student journals publish work by undergraduates in multiple disciplines from any college or university. They include the *Journal of Student Research* (http://www.jofsr.com/index.php/path/index), the *American Journal of Undergraduate Research* (http://www.ajuronline.org/), and the *Journal of Undergraduate Research and Scholarly Excellence* (http://jur.colostate.edu/).

Peer-reviewed academic journals

If your audience is made up of professionals in the field and your purpose is to demonstrate high-level competence as a scholar—perhaps with the goal of attending a selective graduate program in dance—publishing your work in a peer-reviewed journal may be your goal (see Chapter 2 for an explanation of the peer-review process). In that case, your research would have to be not just mentored by a professor but actually a professional collaboration between your faculty mentor and yourself. Publishing in a peer-reviewed journal is the "gold standard," or most prestigious level, of dissemination of scholarly work. UR is not usually considered for such publications unless the work is coauthored with a faculty member, as meeting the standards for such journals usually require expertise in the field that most scholars attain through graduate study and in their academic careers. If you are collaborating with a professor on a shared project, your professor may already be thinking in terms of a peer-reviewed publication. Having papers accepted for such journals is an expectation for university faculty as they seek tenure and promotion; plus most academics enjoy disseminating their work as part of their engagement in the field of study. If a peer-reviewed journal publication is the goal, your professor will likely take the lead as first author, but the expectations for your contributions will likely be demanding. Experts in the field of study are the arbiters of the quality of the research and writing.

Forms of dissemination

Abstract

In order to present your scholarly work you will first need to submit an *abstract*, or summary, of the work. The abstract is the basis for conference organizers vetting your application to present. (Sometimes, though rarely, additional documents such as a personal statement are requested.) If you are accepted to present, your abstract will appear in the conference program.

An abstract is a one-paragraph overview of a project or study. An abstract for a conference may need to be as brief as 60 words or may go as long as 350 words (for NCUR); check the conference's Call for Abstracts for requirements.

Write the abstract after your work is complete, or is at least far enough along that you have initial findings to report or a product to describe. The abstract focuses on results and the significance of the work. It is written in past tense for most disciplines, but can be in the present tense for dance projects. The abstract for a conference presentation should not be written in future tense. (In other words, you should not submit the same abstract if you created one before you began your work, for a research proposal.)

At the top of the page include a thoughtful, interesting, and informative title, with the first letter of each main word capitalized—no quotation marks, italics, or underlining. Be sure to include the name(s) of the author(s). An abstract is usually structured with the following parts:

- Sentences one to two (or more on a longer abstract): context/background/ need. What is the problem, question, need, or important context that prompted your work?
- Sentences two to three: the purpose/focus of the study or project (you can state the purpose explicitly, e.g., "The purpose of this project was to determine ... to examine ... to analyze ... to learn ... to investigate ... to assess ... to research ...to create ...to compose ...").
- The next two to three sentences: statement of the methods or process you undertook in order to fulfill the purpose.
- The rest of the abstract (sentences two to five): explanation of the results of your work (what you discovered or created) and its significance/implications. Consider how your project relates to others' published work. How will other scholars or the discipline overall benefit from your results? If applicable, how could you or other scholars take your study further?

Posters

Academic posters constitute a distinct genre that calls for planning and presentation of ideas in ways very different from essays or oral presentations. A poster should not be designed as a shortened research paper with images added. As with any other text—in any genre or rhetorical situation—posters should be designed with the audience, context, and purpose in mind.

Poster presentations offer certain advantages over traditional modes of presenting dance scholarship. For one, many more presenters and audience members can be accommodated during a single session, as opposed to the panels of just three or four presenters at a time that are typical in oral-presentation sessions and lecture-recitals. So as participation in UR and creative scholarship grows at most institutions, accommodating hundreds of presenters at campus symposia and other conferences will be more feasible with at least some of the arts and humanities students (not just those in the sciences) presenting posters. Another asset of poster presenting is that students are required to think about their work in new ways, including how to articulate it more succinctly and in a different format. Poster presenters not only gain skills in consolidating points into the content of the poster, but also in their "poster talk" or "elevator speech"—the two-to three-minute synopsis of the study they need to have ready to deliver. Preparing posters also helps students develop skills of visual rhetoric and design thinking, as they consider how to represent their points in visually appealing configurations.

The rhetorical situation (audience, context, and purpose) of poster presentations prompt additional considerations. Because of the opportunities for rich one-on-one interactions with audience members, poster presenters should ensure that the research question, purpose of the study, and major findings are immediately clear. If audience members can grasp the main points right away, the interactions can lead to more nuanced discussion. Consider what an engaged audience member needs to understand quickly in order to ask informed questions during the session. At the same time, think about what a casual observer should walk away with after a more brief perusal of the poster. The uniqueness or distinctiveness of the work should be evident.

Research posters usually include the following parts:

- Summary/abstract paragraph
- Brief introductory/contextual info, including the research questions or project goals
- Theory or critical approach of the researcher
- Explanation of the process or methods
- Findings/results/main ideas
- Significance of the work
- Key quotations from primary texts, participants, and/or the research paper, if applicable
- Photos, maps, illustrations, graphs (making up at least one-third of the poster)
- Bibliography, if brief (Long bibliographies can be made available as handouts and/or as shared cloud documents.)

The poster document is usually created as a single PowerPoint slide, set up with the dimensions of the poster. A typical size is 42 inches in width by 36–38 inches in height, though some conferences have smaller boards available and will therefore require smaller posters. The following suggestions are for the structure and design of the poster:

- At the top, include the title, presenter's name, mentor's name, and your university's and/or sponsoring organization's name and logo.
- Below that heading of the title and names, set up three or four equal-sized columns for text and images.
- The text for most of the poster should be in 32–70-point type so that it is readable at a distance of a few feet. The title can be larger (80–100-point), and captions for images can be smaller (22–24-point).
- Use a white or light background; it makes the poster easier to read, and keeping a white background costs less to print because less ink is used.
- Use dark, coordinating colors for the body of the text, headings, borders and lines, etc.
- Align the columns and use text boxes and borders to create neat lines and a sense of order. Avoid "jagged edges" by placing borders around some text boxes and fully justifying text, i.e., aligning it with both margins.
- Follow a logical sequence and structure for reading left to right and top to bottom.
- Maintain consistency in fonts, styles, sizes of text, and width of text boxes.
- Keep some "white space" for ease of reading and visual calm.
- Break up large amounts of text with images that you have permission to use and that are cited. Text should take up less than two-thirds of the poster.
- Make sure that photos and logos are of high resolution. They should not appear pixilated when viewing the poster at 100% zoom.
- Proofread meticulously before sending the document to the printer, and, if possible, ask at least one other person to proofread it too. Minor errors are easy to miss on a computer screen but show up large on a poster.

In addition to these guidelines, we recommend "Poster-making 101" by Prof. Brian Pfohl at Bates College, available online at http://abacus.bates.edu/~bpfohl/posters/#essentials

Oral presentations

Oral presentations include several of the elements of posters. See the bullet points under "Research posters usually include the following parts" above. The images and bibliography can be presented in slides, which accompany most oral presentations. Although the basic elements of academic presentations are present no matter the format, differences in genre between posters and talks require distinct considerations. An oral presentation requires a more formal, planned out, scripted (to some extent) presentation *in the moment*. The content of a poster is mostly fixed, so the live presenting is short and less formal—a few minutes at most with each member of the audience. Oral presenters, however, have a longer time with the audience (usually 10–15 minutes, plus a few minutes for answering audience questions) that is fixed and often strictly enforced; staying focused and organized is essential to completing the presentation in the scheduled session.

Presenters of talks cultivate highly valued skills of public speaking that include effective use of body language, eye contact, and voice projection in addition to the writing and rhetorical skills developed by working on the content. Our best advice for preparing oral presentations is first to think about the engaging presentations you have attended, as well as those that were unsuccessful in maintaining your interest. What have other presenters done to maintain your attention or to turn you off from their presentation? How have you seen slides and other visual aids used effectively and ineffectively during oral presentations? We find with our students that it is easy to identify what has gone poorly in ineffective presentations—everything from the speaker reading straight from notes without making adequate eye contact with the audience, to reading straight from the slides, back facing the audience; from low voice volume to verbal tics and other nervous habits; from misspellings and typos on slides to mispronunciation of important terms. Simply avoiding those goes a long way toward giving a good presentation.

As you prepare your script and slides, consider what a non-expert could reasonably retain without losing interest, while also ensuring that you engage knowledgeable audience members. That balance usually requires briefly defining some key terms and theories before moving straight to the results and significance of your work.

In addition to writing the script and designing slides, oral presenters should prepare for audience questions. Work with your faculty mentor and classmates to brainstorm what kinds of questions you should anticipate and how you will answer them. It is just as helpful to prepare what to say when you do not know the answer to an audience question. There is no shame in acknowledging the limits of your study or explaining that the scope of your work did not encompass what is being asked. If you are prepared for responding you will be far less anxious about difficult questions.

Lecture-recitals

Lecture-recitals are a unique form of presenting scholarship in the performing arts. They include the components and format of an oral presentation, with a performance piece added. A dance lecture-recital we witnessed that sought to capture the challenges and joys of spiritual pilgrimages of Tibetan Buddhists was choreographed with dance techniques inspired by traditional Tibetan dance forms. The student-researcher, who choreographed and performed the dance, first explained, in the lecture portion of the presentation, how she learned the traditional forms in her study abroad and how and why Tibetan Buddhists make spiritual pilgrimages around sacred mountains, seeking to bring about enlightenment. The lecture informed the performance, allowing audience members to enjoy a deeper level of understanding of the spiritual meaning and historical context of the dance.

Performances of choreographed work

The performance of student-scholars' choreographed work is an important arts-based form of dissemination of scholarly work. Usually supported by an artist's statement or program notes in the performance pamphlet, performance is the primary means of sharing the results of creative inquiry in dance. The idea of the on-stage performance itself as the dissemination of scholarship is rooted in performance studies, an inter-disciplinary, theoretical field which considers artistic and cultural performances as means of transmitting knowledge. Academic texts on practice and performance as research and *PARtake: The Journal of Performance as Research* have advanced understanding in higher education about performance as the appropriate product of "scholartistic" work.

Dance performances are often shared in conjunction with a written artist's statement or program notes. An artist's statement is typically two to three para-graphs explaining: (a) how the choreographer and/or performer created the work to be performed; (b) what the work is "about" (i.e., its story, topic, or theme or, in the case of abstract dance, its imagery and/or an explanation of what abstraction means in the world of dance); and (c) the significance of the work (e.g., influences, inspirations) and/or your reasons for creating it. The focus of an artist's statement is on the artist's process, story, inspirations, and purpose.

Program notes, on the other hand, are distinctly focused on the audience. They may summarize the narrative of a dramatic dance or briefly describe the structure and imagery of a more abstract piece, in order to prepare audience members for what they are about to see. Program notes often translate or elucidate a title that is in a foreign language or is conceptual. Former dance critic for *The New York Times*, Jack Anderson (1983) referred to program notes as "verbal overtures for dances" (para. 2). Although Anderson understood that some aficionados of dance would argue that the performance can and should stand on its own, he believed that succinct program notes build a bridge between the "language" of dance and the audience's often-limited experience in that realm. Anderson saw program notes as a form of hospitality, "a gracious invitation" to the dance (para. 13).

Journal articles

The most lasting and academically prestigious method of disseminating scholarly work is through a journal article. If you are considering graduate study in dance, you may be particularly interested in publishing your work in a journal article, as a clear sign of academic rigor and readiness for more advanced scholarly work.

In order to prepare a manuscript of your UR for possible publication, we recommend the following considerations. The first step is to determine early on that publication is your goal so that you orient yourself from the beginning to do work that could be publishable. Writing a publishable paper starts well in advance of the actual writing. Thinking about whether you want to publish your work at the beginning of your research, when you are focusing the topic and research question, is not too soon. That early goal can help you set up a study that takes on something new, interesting, timely, and significant enough to interest journal editors, reviewers, and readers.

You would also need to decide early on what type of paper to write. Full articles of 15–30 pages are the most rigorous and thorough academic papers. They are completed reports of scholarship of importance in the field. Research briefs are much shorter pieces (typically two to eight pages) that summarize the research and highlight the most important findings and implications. Practice-based papers of varying length include scholarly research but focus on community-based or other practitioner work, with implications for people doing work in schools, therapeutic settings, and other places in the community.

Various journals publish certain types of papers and often have particular page-length requirements. Choosing the target journal—the right journal for your work—is therefore important in the early stages as well. It can be difficult to select the right journal unless you are aiming for a campus undergraduate-research journal, so plan to spend some time researching the best option to submit to first. Do not submit your work to more than one journal at the same time. In order to determine whether a journal is the right one for your work is to look at the articles it has recently published. Is yours at a similar level of work and within the scope of what the journal publishes?

Keep in mind the criteria that the reviewers will be using to evaluate your paper. The journal guidelines may include evaluation criteria. If not, questions such as these are fairly typical for academic journals:

- Does the paper contain new and interesting material?
- Are points presented concisely and in a well-organized format?
- Are the methods explained in a way that they can be replicated?
- Are the findings/results presented clearly and convincingly?
- Is the analysis/discussion relevant and insightful?
- Are the implications/conclusions supported by the evidence presented?
- Are the vocabulary, style, and tone at a high level of sophistication?
- Are any figures, tables, and images necessary and well designed?
- Are all sources cited in the text and included in the bibliography?

Pay close attention to the journal's submission guidelines. They generally include detailed expectations for the format of papers, submission procedures, and copyright policies. Most journal editors will not waste time on manuscripts that do not align with the guidelines.

Questions for discussion

1. What are you most apprehensive about prior to presenting?
2. What do you feel you will gain from the experience?
3. How is performance a form of scholarly work?
4. In which written formats will you share your scholarly work in dance: artist statement, program notes, journal articles?

References

Association of American Colleges & Universities. (2015). The LEAP challenge. Retrieved from http://www.aacu.org/sites/default/files/files/LEAP/LEAPChallengeBrochure.pdf

Anderson, J. (1983). Dance view: Program notes should be invitations to the dance. *New York Times*. Retrieved from https://www.nytimes.com/1983/08/14/arts/dance-view-program-notes-should-be-invitations-to-the-dance.html

Bitzer, L. F. (1968). The rhetorical situation. *Philosophy and Rhetoric*, 1, 1–14.

Council on Undergraduate Research. (2011). About CUR. Retrieved from http://www.cur.org/about_cur

Hart Research Associates. (2015). Falling short? College learning and career success. Retrieved from https://www.aacu.org/sites/default/files/files/LEAP/2015employerstudentsurvey.pdf

National Center for Education Statistics. (2017). Employment rates of college graduates. Retrieved from https://nces.ed.gov/fastfacts/display.asp?id=561

Osborn, J., & Karukstis, K. (2009). The benefits of undergraduate research, scholarship, and creative activity. In M. K. Boyd & J. L. Wesemann (Eds.), *Broadening participation in undergraduate research: Fostering excellence and enhancing the impact* (pp. 41–53). Washington, DC: Council on Undergraduate Research.

10

DANCE/MOVEMENT THERAPY

Sharon W. Goodill

Dance/Movement Therapists provide a safe, supportive environment for exploration of life's challenges.

(Goodill, 2016)

Summary

Dance/movement therapy (DMT) is a creative arts therapy specialty discipline and a mind/body integrated approach to counseling and psychotherapy. Expressive and qualitative aspects of movement and dance are emphasized over functional aspects, with overall goals typically focused on psychological, emotional, social and relational health and well-being. Dance/movement therapists combine verbal and non-verbal communication and they build therapeutic relationships which provide a safe, supportive environment for exploration of life's challenges. This chapter offers a brief discussion of purported therapeutic mechanisms of DMT and includes examples from neuroscientific and biological perspectives. The author offers ideas for research inquiry suitable for undergraduate projects.

Definition and description

DMT is a creative arts therapy specialty that is practiced worldwide. It may be referenced with the terms "dance therapy," "dance/movement therapy" or "dance-movement psychotherapy," depending on the country where an author or speaker is situated. DMT is a mind/body integrated approach to counseling and psychotherapy, in which expressive movement and creative processes are used for communication, problem-solving, increasing self-awareness and for reaching other psychosocial and behavioral goals. The American Dance Therapy Association (ADTA) defines DMT as "the psychotherapeutic use of movement to promote emotional, social, cognitive and physical integration of the individual" (ADTA, n.d.). Integration is a key principle and component, which positions DMT in the domain of integrative, holistic health care (Goodill, 2016). While movement and the bodily-felt experience are central to DMT, dance/movement therapists integrate verbal discussion into therapy sessions, so that patients and clients can intentionally transfer discoveries and changes made in the movement process to other areas of everyday life and functioning.

Because movement is available to all living humans throughout the lifespan, the ways that one can apply and offer DMT are many, and the scope of practice for DMT is very broad. DMT is provided in inpatient and outpatient behavioral health programs, in schools (pre-school through university), community health settings, hospitals, senior care facilities, forensic settings, and more. This therapy is given in both group and individual formats.

In the United States, a master's degree is required to practice and to obtain DMT credentials. The ADTA regulates DMT education and the Dance/Movement Therapy Certification Board confers both the entry level credential, R-DMT (Registered Dance/Movement Therapist) and the advanced credential, BC-DMT (Board Certified Dance/Movement Therapist) to qualified individuals. Professional preparation in DMT involves a blend of psychology and counseling with specialized movement studies, and always includes extensive supervised clinical training. Typically education integrates theory, research and practice using a variety of learning methods. The Laban Movement Analysis (LMA) system (including several observational methods stemming from LMA) is central to movement observation, description, analysis, and assessment in DMT. The ADTA website contains more information, videos, documents, and research guides and is recommended as a resource for students who want to learn more about the application, knowledge base, and development of DMT in the United States and abroad.

Physical, mental, and emotional healing

How does DMT work? In many ways, DMT harnesses the non-technical aspects of dance and reshapes those elements into psychotherapeutic forms. Methods include the use of creative movement and improvisation, shared rhythmic action, creating imagery and metaphor with movement, the sharing and modulation of energy, props that evoke and amplify movement ideas, structured dance steps, breath awareness, emotional expression through movement, and more.

DMT combines the health benefits of moderate exercise, with the therapeutic aspects of self-expression and creative activity, all in the context of a supportive relationship with the therapist. In both individual and group DMT a social microcosm is created, and in this interpersonal space clients can experience, practice, and learn new ways of responding to feeling states in themselves, emotional cues from others, and new ways of looking at the challenges in their lives. Clinical methods tend to be rather flexible and responsive to client needs and preferences, with the therapist guiding the sessions in alignment with treatment goals. In DMT, the client's own movement contributions, even if they are very subtle, initiate the improvisatory explorations, and therapists will often move with their clients using a process called "empathic reflection," sometimes developing a tentative or unformed movement expression into conscious awareness and a crystallized, intentional and meaningful non-verbal expression (Sandel, 1993).

Movement is an ongoing process of change. While someone can move in rigid or perseverative ways, movement anywhere in the body can be seen as the manifestation of a life force and can indicate the degree of one's readiness to change. Studies have suggested that when someone is moving with integrated postural and gestural body level involvement, they are tapping into an intrinsic and individual motivational source (Moore & Yamamoto, 2012).

DMT can increase one's capacity for interoception, or the internal sensing of one's body (Hindi, 2012). Body awareness can be kinesthetic, proprioceptive, and interoceptive. People with poor interoception may have difficulty attending to body cues about anxiety, fear, or other emotional states, and may not respond to those states in adaptive ways. This is especially important in the treatment of posttraumatic stress syndrome or PTSD, when the body's alert systems are on overdrive. In DMT, people struggling with the aftermath of traumatic experiences can learn to read their body's messages accurately, so they can titrate and modify their own responses to events in their social and physical environments (Dieterich-Hartwell, 2017).

DMT and the brain

Neuroscience research has revealed several central nervous system processes that may explain the mechanisms of DMT, or how it works. An important series of studies conducted by researchers in Italy, England, and the United States beginning in the mid-1990s, described the "mirror neuron system" or the mirror mechanisms in the brain. As with much research, their studies were originally conducted with animal models, but since have examined similar patterns in humans. In short, motor neurons in the brain will fire when we ourselves move, and the same neurons will also fire when we observe another person moving. This seems to be true even when movement is very small, such as facial displays of emotion, and it seems to be related to our own motor experience (Berrol, 2006). One study compared ballet dancers, capoeira players and people who practice neither movement form. The mirror neurons in ballet dancers reacted more strongly when watching video of ballet, and less when observing capoeira, while the capoeira players showed stronger responses watching capoeira compared to when observing ballet (Corporation for Public Broadcasting, 2005). It is thought that the mirror mechanisms in our brains are the neuromotor template for social learning, social cognition and empathy. Studies are underway to test that hypothesis. DMT methods involve a great deal of moving together in synchrony, often with people facing each other and coming into unison or near unison, sharing postures, gestures, shapes in space, effort qualities, and rhythm. Thus, these findings have implications for understanding why DMT seems to be effective with improving relational and social skills (McGarry & Russo, 2011; Winters, 2008).

Some studies have taken a biological approach and combined outcomes assessment of psychological symptoms with indicators of either neuroendocrine activity or immune system activity (Bojner-Horwitz, Theorell, & Anderberg, 2003; Jeong, Hong, Lee, Park, Kim, & Suh, 2005). These studies support the use of DMT with people who have primary medical illness, and contribute to our understanding of the mind-body integration.

Possible research topics in DMT

Anyone interested in doing research on DMT should begin by looking at the research that has already been done. Several English language scholarly journals publish research, theory and practice works on DMT. These include the *American Journal of Dance Therapy*, the *Journal of Arts in Psychotherapy*, and the *Journal of Body Movement and Dance in Psychotherapy* to name a few.

- Research topics that might be of interest to students of dance may focus on questions of *effectiveness*. Outcome studies can examine whether a course of DMT reduces maladaptive symptoms or behaviors such as depression, anxiety, or disordered eating. Using a strength-based perspective, a research study might investigate whether and how DMT can bring about desired increases in, for example, resilience, coping, positive emotions, academic performance, or social skills. There are hundreds of studies that have looked at treatment outcomes using a variety of research methods ranging from randomized controlled trials to case studies. To carefully review the DMT research about a certain population or about a certain kind of outcome (e.g., mood, body image, coping, self-efficacy, pain) is very worthwhile.
- DMT researchers use many different types of research designs: quantitative, qualitative (e.g., phenomenology, grounded theory), artistic inquiry, mixed method studies, and program evaluation are a few of the more common design types. Some of these can be very elaborate and costly, but case studies of dance used in a therapeutic manner, and literature based research are both viable options for full-time students.
- Survey or interview studies, with professional dance/movement therapists as interviewees could also be done. Research questions could possibly inquire about the therapists' experiences working with different clinical populations, or different techniques they may use, or how DMT methods are adapted for cultural congruence in different countries.
- Many people who come to DMT as a profession have themselves experienced the health potential of dance. A student might want to use artistic inquiry to explore how dance can be therapeutic on a personal level by exploring one's own relationship to dance and carefully look at how dance has changed or improved one's own life and functioning.

Sample abstract from National Council for Undergraduate Research

Rumination

Emma Coombs, Maura Keefe, Department of Dance, State University of New York, Brockport, 350 New Campus Drive, Brockport NY, 14420

"Rumination" is a solo that addresses the concept of anxiety or panic, with attention to the extremes of complete apprehension and limitation. The work was created using the factors of repetition and releasing of weight consistently within a dance. In wanting to stir up some feeling of emotion from the audience, whether positive or negative, the process started with the creation of a thirty second segment of fast-paced repetitive movements. The most common responses from observers at the first showing of the initial draft of the choreography were feelings of anxiety or comedy. Feedback on the work in process suggested that the dancer was some sort of windup toy, moving quickly and falling over to get back up again; however, to others the dancer was restless and anxious, which led to a consideration of an exploration of worry and anxiety. This became the central idea in the research: how can a dance be choreographed to stir feelings of nervousness and address the disorders of anxiety and panic? Disorders such as obsessive compulsive disorder, panic disorder and generalized anxiety disorder are conveyed in this choreography with the constant repetition of steps and the need to perform tasks a certain number of times. With the clear goal, the piece developed with changing the dynamics of a segment or adding a multitude of pauses to allow the audience to process previous information.

Conclusions

Dance/movement therapists combine verbal and non-verbal communication and they build therapeutic relationships that provide a safe, supportive environment for exploration of life's challenges. Undergraduate researchers interested in this topic should review publications that describe completed research, prior to selecting a topic for exploration. The topics and strategies may include questions of effectiveness of treatments; observations and interviews of DMT practitioners who work with specific populations and with specific techniques, or utilize artistic techniques to explore one's own experiences with emotional issues.

Questions for discussion

1. What is DMT?
2. How does one become a dance movement therapist?
3. How does DMT work?
4. What types of research strategies are best and why?
5. Can choreography be useful in exploring emotional issues? Why or why not?

References

American Dance Therapy Association (ADTA). (n.d.). What is Dance/Movement Therapy? Retrieved June 16, 2018 from https://adta.org/faqs/

Berrol, C. F. (2006). Neuroscience meets dance/movement therapy: Mirror neurons, the therapeutic process and empathy. *The Arts in Psychotherapy*, 33(4), 302–315.

Bojner-Horwitz, E., Theorell, T., & Anderberg, U. M. (2003). Dance/movement therapy and changes in stress-related hormones: A study of fibromyalgia patients with video-interpretation. *The Arts in Psychotherapy*, 30(5), 255–264.

Corporation for Public Broadcasting. (2005). NOVA: Research Update: Daniel Glaser's latest study with ballet and capoeira dancers. Retrieved June 16, 2018 from http://www.pbs.org/wgbh/nova/sciencenow/3204/01-resup.html

Dieterich-Hartwell, R. (2017). Dance/movement therapy in the treatment of post traumatic stress: A reference model. *The Arts in Psychotherapy*, 54, 38–46.

Goodill, S. (2016). Dance/Movement Therapy and Integrative Medicine. ADTA Talk. Retrieved from https://www.youtube.com/watch?v=uz6S9LQvvHQ&t=105s&index=4&list=PLrbXrO8yG6hpvRWRnNTij7_CWTt2Th2J

Hindi, F. S. (2012). How attention to interoception can inform dance/movement therapy. *American Journal of Dance Therapy*, 34, 129–140. https://doi.org/10.1007/s10465-012-9136-8

Jeong, Y., Hong, S., Lee, M., Park, M., Kim, Y., & Suh, C. (2005). Dance movement therapy improves emotional responses and modulates neurohormones in adolescents with mild depression. *International Journal of Neuroscience*, 115(12), 1711–1720. https://doi.org/10.1080/00207450590958574

McGarry, L. M., & Russo, F. A. (2011). Mirroring in dance/movement therapy: Potential mechanisms behind empathy enhancement. *The Arts in Psychotherapy*, 38(3), 178–184.

Moore, C. L., & Yamamoto, K. (2012). *Beyond Words: Movement Observation and Analysis*, 2nd ed. London/New York: Routledge.

Sandel, S. (1993). The process of empathic reflection in dance therapy. In S. Sandel, S. Chaiklin, & A. Lohn (Eds.), *Foundations of dance/movement therapy: The life and work of Marian Chace*. Columbia, Maryland: The Marian Chace Memorial Fund of the American Dance Therapy Association.

Winters, A. F. (2008). Emotion, embodiment, and mirror neurons in dance/movement therapy: A connection across disciplines. *American Journal of Dance Therapy*, 30, 84–105. https://doi.org/10.1007/s10465-008-9054-y

11

INTERDISCIPLINARY PROJECTS

Lynnette Young Overby

> Preparing young people to engage in major issues of our times requires that we nurture their ability to produce quality interdisciplinary work.
>
> *(Boix Mansilla & Gardner, 2000)*

Summary

The focus of this chapter is on the topic of interdisciplinarity. The ability to reach beyond one's discipline provides opportunities to develop unique projects that would not be possible with only one disciplinary focus. Undergraduate research programs can promote the development of interdisciplinary projects in formal and informal ways. Dancers can become interdisciplinary scholars by combining dance with another discipline. This is an appropriate strategy for students who are dance minor students, with a different academic major. However, dance majors may also have expertise (more than one major) and be able to make that combination work. Another strategy is to collaborate with a student in another major to develop a project.

Introduction—Interdisciplinary research

The problems that exist in the world will not be solved by one discipline, but by the conscious integration of concepts and skills that cross several disciplines (Boix Mansilla & Gardner, 2000; Boix Mansilla & Duraising, 2007). Interdisciplinary collaborations require knowledge and skill in each discipline. This knowledge may occur in one individual, e.g., the University of Delaware dance minor students who have an academic major, or two or more individuals representing different disciplines working together to solve a particular problem, or create a new artistic work. Many dance scholars have conducted research that crosses disciplines. For example, dance science scholars incorporate knowledge from the discipline of kinesiology. In this chapter, the dance minor capstone, the ArtsBridge Scholar Program and performance-based scholar/artist projects, see Figures 11.1 and 11.2, are shared as possible models for dance interdisciplinarity. Reflections by students are included to illustrate the impact of these programs.

Interdisciplinary projects—University of Delaware

Throughout this book, we share examples of interdisciplinary work conducted by undergraduate students. In this chapter we will first share the dance minor capstone syllabus and reflections by students from the University of Delaware. Next the ArtsBridge Scholars Program and reflections will be described and, lastly, the descriptions and reflections of the scholar/artists performance-based research program will be provided.

The University of Delaware Dance Minor Capstone Course

Course description

This course will provide students, who are completing the dance minor with an opportunity to develop, implement and assess a project that combines content from the dance minor program with their disciplinary major. The project will culminate in a performance or a presentation.

FIGURE 11.1 The Colored Convention (2018)
Choreography: Lynnette Young Overby, with choreographic contributions from the cast. Photo credit: Jessica Eastburn.

FIGURE 11.2 *Prelude* (2018)
Choreography: Lynnette Young Overby, with choreographic contributions from the cast. Photo credit: Jessica Eastburn.

The full semester—45 contact hours will be devoted to this project. An appropriate mentor will guide the student in the completion of the project.

Assignments

Each project will involve the creative process with a focus on integrating two or more disciplines. Choices include the following:

- *Choreographic project*: the choreography may be solo or group. The inspiration/content will illuminate the synthesis of two or more disciplines. The use of multi-media technology is strongly encouraged.

- *Research project*: this project can be: (1) original research on topics for which valid techniques in experimental, historical, ethnographic, clinical or arts-based research have been applied in the collection of data and with appropriate analytical treatment of the data; (2) research reviews on topics of current interest with a substantial research literature base; or (3) theoretical papers presenting well formulated but as of yet untested models.
- *Community engagement project*: the project includes a community partner related to the disciplinary major with a specific problem/need. Co-creation, implementation and evaluation of a movement/dance/arts project will be described in a well-documented report.
- *Teaching project*: the teaching project will include an interdisciplinary focus. The major discipline will be integrated with relevant content from dance as the focus of in depth lessons/units/projects. Teaching may occur in a school or community setting.

Final presentation

The dance capstone experience will be presented at the end of the semester in a public forum:

1. Oral presentation—Pecha Kucha style
2. Final paper

   - Include a cover sheet (title, name, date)
   - Double space the paper (12 point font)
   - Include headings throughout (APA format)

     a. Introduction
     b. Methodology
     c. Findings/results (include tables and/or graphs)
     d. Discussion
     e. Appendix (raw data, lesson plans, survey instruments)
     f. References

The learning outcomes/goals and assessments are set out in Table 11.1.

TABLE 11.1 Components of Dance Minor Capstone Course

Learning outcomes	Activities	Assessment
Synthesis of minor	Website development	Accuracy, completion
Integration of major and minor content	Choreography, research, outreach, or teaching	Mentor evaluationProject evaluation

Reflections by dance minor capstone students

Embodied Cognition & Dance: Does Performing Motor Movement Impact Thinking Task Output?

Melissa Brower, dance minor capstone, University of Delaware, 2018

At first, I was very skeptical in thinking I would never find something in common between the two (dance and cognitive science), but over the course of this project, I've had the opportunity to learn how the art of dance can be applicable to the idea of embodied cognition and the relationship between the body and the mind. In further regards to dance, I believe my project deems to not only encourage others who are unfamiliar with dance to try it out sometime due to its lasting positive impacts, but to also continue confirming a dancer's love for this art and how it can translate into other aspects of life like the thinking process.

The Franklin Method Applied to Improving Dance Technique

Andrea Bianculli, dance minor capstone, University of Delaware, 2013

By integrating my neuroscience major with my dance minor, this capstone project helped me to focus on the science behind dance. I learned that there are many unconventional ways to improve dance technique and that simple meditation can be one of them. Neuroscience research suggests that the brain is constantly changing in order to accommodate for changes in behavior, environment, and neural processes. By using imagery and meditation to visualize improving technique, the brain can change to allow it to control physical movements of the body. This integration of neuroscience with dance was fascinating and I would enjoy doing further research on this topic.

ArtsBridge Scholars Program

The ArtsBridge Scholars Program at the University of Delaware provided a lab like experience where students worked together in a Summer Scholars format to gain knowledge and skills in arts integration, research and teaching. They were required to complete an annotated bibliography, research topics for future arts integration, develop lessons, teach at least one lesson, reflect on that experience and revise the lessons. The students who were a part of the Undergraduate Research Summer Scholars Program, where, along with 400–500 other students, they gained knowledge in ethics, library resources, oral and written communication. An abstract was required and an oral or poster presentation was delivered at the end of the ten-week program.

After the Summer Scholars program, the students were then assigned to schools where they collaborated with classroom teachers, and conducted research arts integration.

Between 2008 and 2016, 40 scholars spent between one and four years as ArtsBridge scholars. They produced seven articles or book chapters, $200,000.00 in grant funding supported the projects, and 12 national and international presentations were delivered. Three Senior Theses were complete. We estimate over 10,000 pre-K-12 students and their teachers were impacted by this program. Next, two former ArtsBridge scholars share their experiences, with other voices included in forthcoming chapters.

Heather Levine, ArtsBridge scholar, University of Delaware, 2008–2011

As an educator-in-training, ArtsBridge allowed me to experience firsthand the importance of interdisciplinary learning. This approach helps students to see connections between disciplines and create more authentic learning experiences. ArtsBridge, in particular, also helped instill the practice of honoring various learning styles and multiple intelligences in the classroom, which can be an invaluable tool for reaching students across achievement gaps. Be it students with learning disabilities, second-language backgrounds, or even just students who learn best actively rather than passively—providing all students with entry points to the curriculum is essential. In my own classroom practice, I consistently strive to utilize these skills in order to engage all learners and keep our learning environment fresh and fun.

Rebecca Hurlock, ArtsBridge scholar, University of Delaware, 2014–2017

During my undergraduate career at the University of Delaware, I had the opportunity to work as an ArtsBridge scholar in order to combine my passions of education and dance. As an Elementary Teacher Education major and a dance minor, I was interested in exploring the benefits that the arts and dance could provide for students at any level. This undergraduate research program gave me the opportunity to work with educators across the state of Delaware, designing lessons plans and activities that integrated movement into a wide range of subject areas. I implemented these activities and analyzed their effectiveness. As I started working in elementary schools as a teacher candidate, I created professional development opportunities for teaching professionals to integrate movement into their daily lessons. Now, as a special education teacher, I continue to utilize these skills to support my students of varied social, emotional, physical, and academic levels.

Scholar/artists

In collaboration with Gabrielle Foreman a literacy historian at the University of Delaware, undergraduate students have been involved in several arts-based research projects focused on African American history. In arts-based research projects, there is an effort to extend beyond the limiting constraints of discursive communication in order to express meanings that otherwise would be ineffable (Barone & Eisner, 2012). By transforming important African American history into an art form and by engaging the community, a broad range of audiences can experience the material. In the case of *Sketches—The Life of Harriet E. Wilson in Dance, Poetry and Music* (Overby, 2012), audiences of university students, secondary school students, and anyone interested in viewing the work on YouTube have access to this work.

The scholar/artists became participant/observers in the creation and performance of these works. They were each assigned a topic area to conduct research. From their research, they created a character and historical time period. In addition to traditional research, the students were required to maintain a journal, and conduct embodied research into the life/times of a particular individual.

The scholar/artists have been integrally involved in all aspects of the productions. To date, four "Performing History" arts-based research projects have been produced with English Professor, P. Gabrielle Foreman and a host of artists. *Sketches—The Life of Harriet E. Wilson in Dance, Poetry and Music* premiered in 2012. Their collaboration continued in 2014 with the premiere of *Dave the Potter* (Overby, 2014), a multidisciplinary work designed to honor the history and creativity of an exceptional enslaved potter and poet, David Drake. In 2016, she produced a multidisciplinary performance/educational project that spanned the countries of the United States and South Africa titled, "*Same Story"—Different Countries* (Overby, 2016). The 2018 arts-based research project is titled *Women of Consequence—Ambitious, Ancillary and Anonymous* (Overby, 2018).

Dominique Oppenheimer, scholar/artist, University of Delaware Summer Scholar, "Same Story" Different Countries, 2015–2017

As a scholar/artist under the direction of Dr. Overby, my experiences in research and performance were invaluable. Going into the nonprofit world through AmeriCorps after my college career, I found that the skills and knowledge gained through these experiences were incredibly useful for learning how to effectively serve the community. The research experience encouraged discipline, mindfulness, and dedication both in the library and in the dance studio. Undergraduate research in the dance realm taught me about recognizing and building connections between different fields, creative problem-solving, being adaptable, honoring and sharing diverse histories and perspectives, tying together factual research with artistic concepts, using unexpected mediums to approach important subjects and stories, and communicating ideas to a wide variety of audiences. As I've worked with other AmeriCorps members this past year, I have been able to share what I've learned regarding the tools of interdisciplinary learning in order to raise awareness of its benefits and possibilities.

Ikira Peace, scholar/artist, "Same Story" Different Countries *and* Women of Consequence, 2014–2018

This project has been my first door in using my voice and stepping further away from silence. It fertilized a spirit in me, that I believe many of my people can have trouble latching on to. Living in this spirit, I found a leader. I found my passion. I gave birth to a voice that will be active the rest of my life.

Suggestions for possible interdisciplinary capstone projects involving dance

- Create a series of compositions based on a series of paintings by a visual art major
- Examine correlations between science experiments and creation of original choreography
- Focus on a social issue – create a dance that promotes a deeper understanding of the topic
- Analyze the role of dance in television advertisements
- Study the pattern of dance related injuries, and/or their prevention
- Study the effects of mindfulness-based stress reduction on performance
- Collaborate with a physics student to create a choreographic work
- Collaborate with a policy student to design a policy document regarding dance education in a particular location
- Collaborate with an anthropologist to determine the existence of dance in ancient populations.
- Conduct a literature review on number and types of research studies related to dance and disabilities

Assessment of interdisciplinary projects

Assessment of interdisciplinary projects should focus on qualities of interdisciplinary understanding, e.g., the purpose of the project, the inclusion of disciplinary components, and a reflective component to discern a student's critical awareness (see Figure 11.3).

Conclusion

Interdisciplinary approaches to dance research provide the opportunity to think beyond the boundaries of a discipline. Three approaches from the University of Delaware, shared in this chapter included, the Dance Minor Capstone, The ArtsBridge Scholars Program and scholar/artists projects, which are examples of formal programs that can support and facilitate the development, implementation and assessment of interdisciplinary projects that include dance and at least one other discipline.

Discussions/applications

1. Which disciplines are appropriate to combine? Why?
2. How do you develop respectful relationships that acknowledge the strengths of each discipline?
3. What are the benefits and challenges of conducting interdisciplinary projects?
4. Application: design an interdisciplinary project.

Criteria	Guiding Questions
I. Disciplinary grounding	Are the selected disciplines appropriate to inform the issue at hand? Are any key perspectives or disciplinary insights missing? Are the considered disciplinary theories, examples, findings, methods, and form of communication accurately employed, or does the work exhibit misconceptions?
II. Advancement through integration	Where is there evidence of disciplinary integration (e.g., conceptual framework, graphic representation, model, leading metaphor, complex explanation, or solution to a problem)? Is there evidence that understanding has been enriched by the integration of different disciplinary insights?
III. Critical awareness	Does the work show a clear sense of purpose, framing the issue in ways that invite an interdisciplinary approach? Is there evidence of reflectiveness about the choices, opportunities, compromise, and limitations involved in interdisciplinary work and about the limitations of the work as a whole?

FIGURE 11.3 Summary of key criteria and guiding assessment questions. Reprinted with permission: Boix Mansilla, & Duraising, 2007.

References

Barone, T., & Eisner, E. (2012). Arts-based research. Thousand Oaks, CA: SAGE Publications Inc.

Boix Mansilla, V., & Duraising, E. W. (2007). Targeted Assessment of Students' Interdisciplinary Work: An Empirically Grounded Framework Proposed. *The Journal of Higher Education*, 78(2), 215–237. Retrieved from http://www.jstor.org/stable/4501203

Boix Mansilla, V., & Gardner, H. (2000). On disciplinary lenses and interdisciplinary work. In S. Wineburg, & P. Grossman (Eds.) *Interdisciplinary Curriculum Challenges of Implementation* (pp. 161–198). New York: TC Press.

Overby, L. (2012). Sketches—The Life of Harriet E. Wilson in Dance, Poetry and Music. Lauren Wells, composer, Glenis Redmond, poet, Gabrielle Foreman, literary historian. First performed, March, 2012, Mitchell Hall, Univeristy of Delaware. Retrieved from http://www.youtube.com/watch?v=RJgWgL9Zb4A

Overby, L. (2014). Dave the Potter. Ralph Russell, composer, Glenis Redmond, poet, Gabrielle Foreman, literary historian. First performed, March 2014, Mitchell Hall, University of Delaware. Retrieved from https://www.youtube.com/watch?v=4G8pz4cBDGs (Field Cotton—Excerpt

Overby, L. Y. (2016). "Same Story"—Different Countries. Collaborators include Group of South African musicians, and Ralph Russell, composer, Glenis Redmond, poet, Garth Erasmus, visual artist. First performed, March 2016, Baby Grand Theatre, Wilmington, DE. Retrieved from https://sites.udel.edu/ss-dc/

Overby, L. Y. (2018). Women of Consequence—Ambitious, Ancillary and Anonymous. Ralph Russell, composer; Glenis Redmond, poet, Gabrielle Foreman, literary historian. First performed, March 2018, Baby Grand Theatre, Wilmington, DE.

Veronica Boix, Mansilla, & Elizabeth Dawes, Duraising. (2007). Targeted Assessment of Students' Interdisciplinary Work: An Empirically Grounded Framework Proposed. *The Journal of Higher Education*, 78(2), 215–237. Retrieved from http://www.jstor.org/stable/4501203

12

PUBLIC SCHOLARSHIP AND DANCE

Lynnette Young Overby

> To give real service you must add something, which cannot be bought or measured
> with money, and that is sincerity and integrity.
>
> *(Douglas Adams, https://www.brainyquote.com/topics/service)*

Summary

This chapter opens with an introduction to engaged scholarship with definitions and descriptions. Engaged scholarship in dance involves development, implementation, and assessment of scholarly projects that are mutually beneficial to the community partner and the researcher. Specific guidelines are provided on how to create a scholarly engagement project with a community partner. The chapter follows with specific examples by undergraduate students and a list of potential topics and resources.

Introduction

Many undergraduate students want to conduct research that will make a difference in the lives of community members. Engaged scholarship is both a methodology and an approach to move beyond a volunteer activity to a fully engaged and impactful project that will address critical issues.

Engaged scholarship in dance involves development, implementation, and assessment of scholarly projects that are mutually beneficial to the community partner and the researcher. Examples from choreography, teaching and research will be described.

Definition of community engagement and engaged scholarship

Boyer, in 1996, gave us a new way to view scholarship—that scholarship was not relegated to findings from a laboratory or in a best-selling novel, but that scholarship could make a difference in our immediate communities and beyond:

The academy must become a more vigorous partner in the search for answers to our most pressing social, civic, economic, and moral problems, and must reaffirm its historic commitment to what I call the scholarship of engagement.

(Boyer, 1996, p. 11)

This revelation has influenced higher education in a variety of ways, and especially in our view of engaged scholarship. Engaged scholarship is scholarship that has as an outcome, the application of knowledge to a societal problem. The engaged scholars complete projects and disseminate findings that influence community knowledge and collaboratively develop solutions to problems.

Although engaged scholarship varies with the purpose, outcome and structure:

All engaged scholarship should adhere to the definition provided by the Carnegie Foundation for the Advancement of Teaching, which posits that Community Engagement is a collaboration between institutions of higher education and their larger communities (local, regional/state, national, global) for the mutually beneficial exchange of knowledge and resources in a context of partnership and reciprocity.

(Carnegie Foundation, n.d.)

In a recent publication titled: *Public Scholarship in Dance* (Overby, 2016), examples of community engaged teaching, research, service, and choreography are provided.

Public Scholarship in the Undergraduate Curriculum

The undergraduate student has opportunities to take part in course-based research in the form of a class project or as a major capstone or senior thesis.

The dance projects may focus on dance only or be an interdisciplinary exploration. Co-curricular opportunities such as the University of Delaware Summer Scholars Undergraduate Research Program, or projects that are a part of student organizations can be the catalyst for community engagement projects

Components of a scholarly engagement project

Undergraduate students will work closely with their faculty mentors (the university partners) in all aspects of the engaged scholarship project.

1. In developing projects that fall into the category of engaged scholarship, the university partners, will first determine the assets and challenges that exist in a particular community setting.
2. Next, the university partners will focus on the specific aspects of dance and/or another academic area that will work in concert with the community assets, and address the challenges. A project will be co-created with goals and outcomes developed together with the community partner.

3. The outcomes should address specific community needs and foster academic and personal growth in the scholar.
4. From the beginning until the conclusion of the project, each partner should review goals and make certain a balance between academic and community goals are achieved.
5. Assessment will be co-designed by the community partner and the university partners and should be implemented in a formative manner.
6. A summative project assessment will provide important information about the benefits, challenges and next steps of the project for both the community partner and the scholar.
7. Lastly, the outcomes of the project should be disseminated to the appropriate stakeholders.

CREATING ENGAGED SCHOLARSHIP PROJECTS IN DANCE

Step one: Identifying shared interests, potential partners and possible projects

- Project emerges in context of mutual interests, needs, and abilities

Step two: Establishing a plan that fulfills community and university interests

- Partners have a clear understanding of the project's objectives, timetable, and mode of communication
- Partners have determined an equitable allocation of time and resources
- Partners have a formal agreement about leadership and work roles
- Issues of trust, information, and responsibility are balanced

Step three: Foster reciprocity and mutual recognition

- Partners have on going in-depth discussions to consider whether the project's objectives, processes, outcomes, are meeting the needs of each partner
- Efforts to ensure reciprocity, mutual recognition and reward are ongoing

Step four: Assessment guides decision making about projects

- A formative and summative assessment processes guide decisions about current and future project development

Step five: Laying the foundations for continued engagement and dissemination of outcomes

- Partners formally and informally consider ways to improve
- Partners formally disseminate project outcomes

Abstracts: Engaged Scholarship in Dance—Dance Capstone Projects University of Delaware

Math is music to our ears: The effects of a music and movement integrated mathematics curriculum on second grade students' engagement with learning

Amanda Bocarrdi, senior thesis, University of Delaware

The purpose of this mixed methods research study was to show the effect, if any, that instruction of mathematics through a music and movement integrated curriculum has on second grade students' emotional, behavioral, and cognitive engagement with learning. Two theories that are imperative in the study of education are the Experiential Learning Theory and the Theory of Student Engagement. According to the Experiential Learning Theory, when students fully experience subject matter, they will grasp a better understanding of the material and remember it. One way that students are able to learn through doing is through the arts of music and dance. Learning through these art forms engages students emotionally, behaviorally, and cognitively. Throughout the United States, student disengagement is high, especially in mathematics classrooms, and there has been a decline in arts programs over the past several decades. The curriculum supplement "Math is Music to Our Ears" provides an alternative way to incorporate art-driven creativity into standard curriculum content through an arts-integrated approach to instruction. After completing preliminary research on arts-integration techniques and utilizing the Common Core State Standards for mathematics and national core arts standards for music and dance, a second grade mathematics curriculum was created to integrate music and dance into mathematics instruction. The curriculum supplement consisted of six lessons covering the areas of: (a) time, (b) money, (c) fractions, (d) rhythm, and (e) basic skills in creative movement. A group of seventeen second grade participants at a public school in Newark, Delaware were instructed with this curriculum. Quantitative and qualitative data on the students' emotional, behavioral, and cognitive engagement were collected, including journal reflections, surveys, videotaped student performances, and written work samples. Consistent with prior research on arts integration, the students demonstrated high levels of emotional, behavioral, and cognitive engagement. In terms of emotional engagement, student journals and surveys indicated that between 76% and 90% of the students' responses reflected high enjoyment and enthusiasm. In terms of behavioral engagement, student performances and journals showed that between 77% and 98% of the scores indicated high levels of attention, effort, and persistence in each category. Finally, in terms of cognitive engagement, student work samples showed that 94% of the students could accurately synthesize ideas across math and the arts, which indicated deep cognitive processing. Thus, based on these results, integrating music and movement into mathematics curricula is a unique approach that can help engage students with learning.

Learning about the body through movement: teaching body systems through dance concepts in a 1st grade classroom

Rachel Austin, dance capstone, University of Delaware, 2016

This project aimed to qualitatively and quantitatively analyze the effects of arts integration on first grade students' ability to memorize and understand the circulatory system, nervous system, and digestive system. By integrating qualitative biology with dance, I came up with a lesson plan in a 1st grade classroom to teach about the circulatory, nervous, digestive systems. The arts integration project took place at Kathleen H. Wilbur Elementary School in Bear, DE, in the classroom of Mr. David O. and 24 students. Before the lesson each week, a pre-test was distributed, where students answers a few quick questions. The lesson spanned a duration of 30–50 minutes, which included overviews of dance and the body system, as well as activities for both the art and science concept separately and combined. The lesson finished with choreography to physically and visually depict the body system being taught that day and recorded to analyze the student's engagement, behavior and knowledge. Once the lesson was finished, students answered the same questions prior to the lesson to test for increase of knowledge. Limitations to this study included no control group and inconsistent attendance. Mr. O. noted the lessons seemed successful but noticed there may be a lack of connection between dance and the body system being portrayed. Through the videos, teacher's observations and post test, students were shown to increase their knowledge after the arts integrated lesson with more engagement and enthusiasm than a traditional lecture. Overall, as found in other works, arts integration had a large effect on the student's engagement, attentiveness, enjoyment, and understanding of the topic (Gilbert, 1992). In terms of choosing dance as the art form to integrate with body systems, dance has a large impact on children's development through both physical activity and as an outlet for self-expression, allowing children to explore and create and claiming that the arts are the connective tissue that keeps our mind and body intact (Dow, 2010) Through this non-traditional teaching strategy, an increase in reasoning, perspective-taking, questioning and investigating, observing and describing, comparing and connecting new ideas to past knowledge occurred in a majority of the students, as previously found in other studies (Vega, 2012). In the future, I hope that arts integrated lesson plans will be implemented in all schools to better engage students and help them to conceptualize complex biological mechanism. I also hope that websites can be developed to share arts integrated lesson plans between teachers to better help teachers with little experience in the arts to add arts integration into their classrooms.

Balance exercises for individuals 65 and older

Allison Blackwell, dance minor capstone, University of Delaware, 2016

Individuals over the age of 65 have an increased risk of falling. This is a topic that Exercise Science majors are commonly faced with as a problem. Not only do falls have a physical consequence leading to health concerns, they also contain a mental component. After a fall has been sustained, individuals can become scared of carrying out their everyday activities which can further lead to a decreased quality of life.

For my project, I chose to utilize balance exercises and stretches commonly taught and incorporated in dance to aid in fall prevention in an elderly population.

I was fortunate enough to have 5 women from the Holy Family's Women's Group agree to have me teach a lesson at one of their monthly meetings. After researching statistics regarding falls in the elderly population, as well as balance exercises and stretches that have been found helpful in reducing the risk of falling, I was able to design my project. I began by giving the 5 women a "pre-test" of their current knowledge regarding the likelihood of falls in the elderly population as well as their comfort level of having a fall themselves. I then provided the individuals with a packet, which included the statistics I have gathered regarding falls in a clearly laid out format. It also included the definitions of static and dynamic balance. The next portion of the educational experience consisted of 5 balance exercises and stretches that I had compiled from research, which have been found to aid in fall prevention. I informed the women they could watch as I demonstrated the stretches and exercises in front of them. I also allowed them, if they were interested and felt comfortable, to join in at any time. All five women decided to join in with me during the 5 exercises. Finally, the women took a "post-test" where they were able to provide me with information regarding what they felt they had learned and if they thought they would continue to utilize the exercises I had provided with them at home. Lastly, I provided each woman with a credit card sized list of the exercises that would be easy and simple to carry around with them or to leave by their bedside with the hopes of the women truly utilize the exercises. The results indicated a gain in knowledge regarding exercises designed to help with balance. After the educational experience, all of the women expressed to me how grateful they were for the lesson. All five women felt as though they had learned something new regarding falls and their own risk level of experiencing a fall. Some of the responses included, "I was unaware that exercise could be used as a preventative strategy to avoid falls." Another response read, "Being over the age of 65, I did not realize that I am now at an increased risk for falling. I am glad to have learned that I can use balance strategies as a method to prevent future falls." As a dancer, I have a unique background where I truly value the importance of balance exercises and stretches. Elderly individuals can benefit from this knowledge to maintain or improve balance to prevent a fall.

Suggested research topics for engaged scholarship in dance

- Develop a policy regarding the need for dance in a community by creating a literature review and disseminating the material to policy makers.
- In collaboration with a dance therapist create a project that utilizes dance exercises for a patient with a mental illness. At the conclusion of the project, send the activities to the therapist and patient.

- Focus on the area of eating disorders in dancers. Collaborate with a studio owner to design informational materials that will inform the parents and students about specific eating disorders.
- In collaboration with a pre-school teacher, design a project that utilizes dance to develop student's ability to transform mathematical concepts into body movement.
- In collaboration with a state arts organization, develop a survey to learn about the types of preferred dance experiences in various parts of the state.
- Collaborate with a music student and an environmental science major to create an interdisciplinary choreographic project with a focus on environmental science, dance and music. Plan to share this work with middle school students
- Conduct a survey to determine the nutritional practices of students majoring in dance. Use information appropriate nutritional practices or active dancers to design a web based educational program university level dancers.

Conclusion

Engaged scholarship can be another option for students who are interested in applying their knowledge in a real world setting. The project should be co-created, co-implemented, co-assessed, and co-disseminated with a community partner.

Questions for discussion

1. What are the criteria for assessing community partnerships?
2. What projects have the most potential and why?
3. What is the difference between service learning and community engagement?

References

Boyer, E. (1996). The scholarship of engagement. *Journal of Public Service and Outreach*, 1(1), 11–20.

Carnegie Foundation. (n.d.). Carnegie Community Engagement Classification. Retrieved from https://compact.org/initiatives/carnegie-community-engagement-classification/

Overby, L. (2016). *Public Scholarship in Dance*. Champaign, Illinois: Human Kinetics.

13

CHOREOGRAPHY AS ORIGINAL RESEARCH

Lynnette Young Overby

> When I choreograph, I never use people merely to create a design. I mean, abstraction is always present in an art form, and I use it, but I have never used human beings simply as a design element. My work has always been concerned with humanity, in one way or another. Basically, I feel the beauty in man is in his diversity, and in his deep inner feelings.
>
> *(McKayle, 1973)*

Summary

Choreography is an important option for undergraduate students interested in dance research. Although the research terminology is steeped in science disciplines, the process of creating a new choreographic work has similar components. Students may conduct research through traditional means or through an embodied, improvisational approach. Students may document their process of choreography in various ways including by writing an artist statement, or by producing a formal paper. In this chapter, examples from the University of Delaware Dance Minor Capstone course and from national conferences are included.

Introduction

Choreography is also considered research in dance. The stages of choreography are very similar to any other creative project. First, background information is gathered to begin the choreographic journey through traditional text-based work, or through embodied improvisational work or both; next, the work is set, after revising and editing the work and through the application of choreographic forms. The final product—the dance—is next, and dissemination occurs via performance, or film, allowing the choreographer to share the final output with audiences. As a requirement of the Dance Minor Capstone course at the University of Delaware, students who choose choreography as their project, write a formal paper on the process.

In this chapter, the process of choreographic research will be revealed, followed by the development of an artist statement, examples of interdisciplinary choreography dance capstone projects, samples of abstracts submitted to the National Conference on Undergraduate Research (NCUR) and suggestions for choreographic research.

How to document the process?

Documenting the process of choreography may take place by: (a) writing an artist statement, as an example from St. Olaf College shares; or (b) through writing a formal paper about the process, as completed by students at the University of Delaware; or (c) through an abstract of the work, as indicated in abstracts presented at national conferences. Documentation and dissemination of the work may also occur as a film or a notated score.

Writing an artist statement

Artist statements from senior capstone students at St. Olaf

Senior Dance Project Artist Statement Information and Guidelines are provided for students who are a part of the dance program at St. Olaf University (Choreographic and Performance Project Options) (St. Olaf, 2012).

What is an artist statement?

An artist statement is a written document, typically by the artist, that succinctly describes his or her artistic work. The artist statement is typically displayed alongside the artist's work at an exhibition or performance.

The senior dance project artist statement

Your senior dance project artist statement will examine your process as a choreographer or performer, depending upon your project option, during the creation and implementation of your senior project. Your artist statement will also place your current work in the context of your previous body of work as a dance major at St. Olaf College. The final draft of your artist statement will be displayed in the lobby of the performance space in conjunction with your final project performance.

Artist statement directions

Your artist statement must be written in paragraph form not exceeding 250 typed words, using Times 14pt. font. Include the title of your project as a heading for the statement and your name.

Within your statement, you must address the following questions:

For the choreographic project option:

1. What was your original intention/inspiration "spine" for this work?
2. What is the prevalent theme/idea of the finished work, and how has it has evolved from the original "spine"?
3. What was your creative process like, from conception to completion?
4. In viewing your work, what elements specifically point an audience member toward an understanding of the theme of the work?
5. How does this work compare/contrast to your previous work?
6. What artistic struggles, successes and discoveries have you encountered in your choreographic process from the beginning of your time at St. Olaf through this point in the completion of your senior project?
7. How have your previous hurdles, successes and discoveries impacted your process and creative process for this particular work?
8. What have you discovered about yourself as a choreographic artist and art making during this process?

For the performance project option:

1. What was your original intention/inspiration ("spine") for this work?
2. What were your intentions/goals in selecting this dance artist to work with and/or work to perform?
3. How would you compare/contrast you approach to this performance process with your previous performance work?
4. How did your role as a performer influence the theme and direction of the piece?
5. What artistic struggles, successes and discoveries have you encountered in your performance process from the beginning of your time at St. Olaf through this point in the completion of your senior project?
6. How have your previous hurdles, successes and discoveries impacted your process and performance of this particular dance?
7. What have you discovered about yourself as a performing artist in this format (electronic, hard copy) you should submit your artist statement?

Artist statement assessment

Your artist statement will be assessed on the degree to which it:

1. Responds to the questions listed in the directions above.
2. Demonstrates appropriate, effective and correct written communication skills.

The artist statement provides a format for choreographers and performers to document their process and reflect on the product.

Interdisciplinary compositions: Perspectives from student choreographers

The dance minor students at the University of Delaware may select choreography as the focus of an interdisciplinary project. Along with the choreography, each student must write a final paper. The paper is in the same format as reports by students who chose to conduct a research, teaching or engagement project for their capstone project.

Final paper format—Dance Minor Capstone Course, University of Delaware

- Include a cover sheet (title, name, date)
- Double space the paper (12-point font)
- Include headings throughout (APA format)

    a.   Introduction
    b.   Methodology
    c.   Findings/results (include tables and/or graphs)
    d.   Discussion
    e.   References
    f.   Appendix (raw data, lesson plans, survey instruments)

For the conclusion of the final paper, the student reflected on their ability to combine their major with their dance minor. Many also commented on the impact of this work on their future. The assessment for the dance minor capstone included the final paper, an oral presentation and a website (the Appendix includes a copy of the assessment form used with all dance capstone students).

Because the students were matriculating through a dance minor program, they completed interdisciplinary choreography projects. The last section of the final paper included a discussion/reflection. Here are three of the reflections by dance minor capstone students Haley Faragher, Ben Dutton and Alexis Trench.

Reflections—Living with anorexia: A story told through dance

Haley A. Faragher, psychology major, dance minor, University of Delaware

Haley was very concerned about the issue of anorexia. She researched the topic, choreographed a dance and created a short film to shine a light on anorexia nervosa and spread awareness as her dance capstone project. She included a pre and post assessment to determine what was gained through this viewing. Her reflection on the project follows:

My main goal was to educate others about anorexia nervosa, share treatment information, touch the hearts of my viewers, and inspire them to reach out to those suffering and spread awareness themselves. After reading all of the recorded responses, I feel that I achieved my goal. After I gathered several responses through the pre-test and post-test in google forms, I decided to upload my short film to YouTube and share it on Facebook as well. The positive responses were immediate on Facebook and my friends began sharing my video on their timelines too. Soon various users that I did not know even shared the video with their friends, and the video is still being shared all over Facebook today. I am so grateful for everyone's efforts in sharing my video and I am elated that my dance minor capstone project has achieved the success that I had genuinely hoped for.

(Faragher, 2016a, 2016b)

Synthesizing dance and music through animal mating rituals

Benjamin Dutton, vocal music major, dance minor, and Alexis Trench, animal science major, dance minor, University of Delaware

Ben Dutton and Music major and Dance Minor collaborated with another Alexis Trench who was an animal science major and Dance minor. Together, they created a project that combined vocal performance and animal mating dances. They choreographed a series of animal mating rituals to classical art songs. The animals were the peacock, guinea fowl and the fly. The music for the project included two pieces by Maurice Ravel from his song cycle *histoires naturelles*, "Le paon" and "La pintade." The third piece was by Max Reger called "Die Bienen."

Ben's reflection:

I was able to learn about the music creation process. One major learned piece for me was that most dances are created once the music is selected, however, the process can be reversed for a whole other artistic effect. Animal behavior can be used to help humans understand the impact that their interactions with animals can have on them. I learned about music production and the complex process that goes into that. I put a lot of what I learned about the choreographic process into practice. It really rounded out all of the components of my undergraduate education and taught me a little extra knowledge before graduation. Some things I think may enhance my work would be to see if an audience might have a greater understanding of mating dances as a result of watching our videos. It could be of use to an elementary school or middle school lesson on animal behavior for a person whose major is Agricultural Education.

(Dutton, 2016)

Alexis' reflection:

> Overall this project opened my eyes in more ways than I had anticipated whilst talking about blue-footed boobies with my friend last summer. I found a major connection between dance and animal behavior. I put a lot of what I learned about the choreographic process into practice. Understanding mating dances might help people to not interrupt this important part of the circle of life to prevent species endangerment and extinction.
>
> *(Trench, 2016)*

Samples of abstracts submitted to the NCUR

Dance as a way of communication and change: Raising awareness on human trafficking through the arts

Whitney Collins (Faculty Mentor: Monica Campbell), Department of Dance, Utah Valley University, 800 W University Pkwy, Orem, UT 84058

Human trafficking is a significant socio-political issue that forces individuals into labor and/or sex slavery. People can become susceptible to human trafficking through various ways, such as: immigration, being a foreign language speaker, living in poverty, being a runaway, and more. Because this illegal act happens in secrecy, and is undoubtedly complex, it is difficult for individuals to grasp the entirety of human trafficking (Fedina). Since it is well hidden, researchers are unable to get exact numbers for exploitation. Estimations for trafficked individuals within the United States ranges between 5,166–60,476 victims (Fedina, 2014). Not only is there an apparent need for more research to be conducted, but there is also a higher need to raise awareness on human trafficking. Although dance is often overlooked, it is one of many tools that can be used to raise awareness. The way dance communicates specific material to an audience is through live performances, visual and rhythmic engagement, and the way dance evokes emotion through powerful movement. Consequently, dance is one of many tools that can reflect on socio-political issues. Research has been conducted through many spectrums ranging from personally choreographing a piece that responds to the subject matter, researching and critically analyzing other choreographers who are raising awareness on human trafficking, and reading printed/online source materials that pertain to the subject matter. This presentation will dive deeper into how the arts facilitate in communicating current socio-political issues relating to human trafficking.

Scholarly research on dance technique

Alicia Garrity (Faculty Mentor: Nola Nolen-Holland), Dance Department, Slippery Rock University, 1 Morrow Way, Slippery Rock, PA 16057

The American Dance festival is a premiere modern dance festival that offers a variety of dance training from videography to choreography. The purpose of this project, "Scholarly Research on Dance Technique," was to conduct in depth research on a variety of modern dance techniques by attending the American Dance Festival. This prestigious festival was six weeks long and consisted of three technique classes a day for five days a week. Through a daily journal of class observations, faculty surveys and by recording personal feedback I received from instructors, I was able increase my understanding of different modern dance techniques. From my summer research I created a choreographic project, which is a five-minute modern dance solo. This part of the project allowed me to embody the different styles and express my interpretation of them. At the festival, I studied two different techniques as well as took a repertory class based on another technique. Each day I recorded data on movement combinations, personal feedback, teaching methods, specific elements of the style and choreographic processes. I found that each style was different; yet, they were all similar in certain ways. My power point presentation will show the similarities and differences between each technique. It will also consist of two different teaching methods. I will also share the choreographic process of Dr. Pearl Primus as taught by SRU professor Ursula Payne. The creative project enhanced my understanding of each technique in a different way. With my data from my research I translated the information into physical movements. I took the specific elements of each style and re-created them, adapting them to fit my body. This part was the most challenging but developed my overall artistry as a dancer. Overall, this project opened my eyes to the world of modern dance. It gave me the opportunity to study with other professionals as well as develop personal contacts that I can reference in the future. It also enhanced my understanding of choreography, professionalism and dance education. For the completion of this project I received a $500 grant from Slippery Rock University. I also received matching scholarships from the American Dance Festival and the SRU Dance Department as well as a summer study scholarship through the Dance Department. The rest of the funding came from my personal account. The project will be submitted to the April 2011 Slippery Rock University Symposium for student research. The creative project will also be adjudicated to be performed on the SRU Dance Department's Fall and Winter Concerts.

Potential choreography topics and strategies

- Collaborate with a visual artist on a specific topic

- Choreograph a work focusing on various choreographic tools, e.g., theme and variation, ground base, canon
- Choreograph a work to poetry
- Choreograph with a focus on the elements of dance, e.g., space, time, force
- Use improvisation as an impetus to choreography
- Create a multidisciplinary work with content from several disciplines
- Create a work focused on a current issue, e.g., Black Lives Matter, Me Too, gun violence
- What you see, hear, touch, and experience can be used as content for choreography
- Create a chance dance

Conclusion

Choreography is a viable option for undergraduate dance students. By utilizing a format that allows documentation and reflection, the choreography becomes an opportunity to develop multiple skills, e.g., creating, writing, and reflecting. The students experience professional growth and build their confidence for future projects.

Questions for discussion

1. Why is it necessary to write an artist's statement?
2. Why should choreography be considered research?
3. What is the benefit of arts-based research?
4. How do I get my choreography adjudicated?
5. Activity: select and research a current issue. Storyboard a beginning, middle, and ending. Improvise on the selected themes, then choreograph the beginning section.

References

Dutton, B. (2016). Synthesizing Dance and Music through Animal Mating Rituals. (Unpublished manuscript). Dance Minor, University of Delaware, Newark, DE.

Faragher, H. (2016a). Living with Anorexia: A Story Told Through Dance. (Unpublished manuscript). Dance Minor, University of Delaware, Newark, DE

Faragher, H. (2016b). Video. Anorexia: A Glimpse. Retrieved from https://www.youtube.com/watch?v=fd6qv4V9vRY

Fedina, L. (2014). Use and Misuse of Research in Books on Sex Trafficking: Implications for Interdisciplinary Researchers, Practitioners, and Advocates. *Trauma, Violence, and Abuse*, 16(2), 188–198. https://doi.org/10.1177/1524838014523337

McKayle, D. (1973) Interview by John Gruen, November 4. Retrieved from https://www.nytimes.com/1973/11/04/archives/with-raisin-he-rises-to-the-top-donald-mckayle-triumphs-as.html

Trench, A. (2016). Synthesizing Dance and Music through Animal Mating Rituals. (Unpublished manuscript). Dance Minor, University of Delaware, Newark, DE. Retrieved from http://www.stolaf.edu/depts/dance/faculty/anthony/courses/Syllabi/_2012-13/Dance_399_F2012_Web_Files/Artist_Statement_Assignment-dance-399-2012.htm

Appendix

Scoring guide oral capstone project and reflection paper

Name: _____

Title: _____

Design			
Contains multiple elements such as text, graphics, sound, video and animation	5	3	1
Contained all presentation elements: Introduction, body, conclusion	5	3	1
Navigation is easy and understandable	5	3	1
Content			
Information is relevant and interesting	5	3	1
Creativity used in design	5	3	1
Demonstration of complete understanding of presented material	5	3	1
Material is clearly referenced	5	3	1
Presentation			
The presentation is fluent from beginning to end	5	3	1
There is an overall synthesis of the presentation	5	3	1
Oral Presentation contains—motivation and lessons learned	5	3	1
Eye contact, vocal level appropriate	5	3	1
Time limit met (5 minutes)	5	3	1
Written reflection			
Introduction—Clearly describes how project was selected. Describes relationship of project to course material	30	20	10

Written reflection			
Description—Procedures and results are clearly described	30	20	10
Conclusion/Applications include information about what was learned from this experience and future applications	30	20	10
Organization/Grammar	10	5	1

Total Score: _____

Additional Comments: _____

Evaluator: _____

14

CULTURAL STUDIES IN DANCE

Lynnette Young Overby

By Looking at ourselves in our infinite human variety, we can better understand our own forms of dance expression and examine unconscious assumptions about them...A comparative perspective is often a mind stretcher, prejudice–dissolver, and taste–widener.
(Hanna, 1989, p. 219)

Summary

Throughout time, all cultures have danced as an integral part of life. When we explore various cultures, we become aware of the direct link between dance and life. This chapter will include information about how researchers have explored various aspects of culture through qualitative research methodologies. Dance ethnography will be explained with examples from the literature. The chapter continues with sample projects conducted by undergraduate students, potential topics for future research and discussion questions.

Introduction

Dance scholars assure us that one can understand a particular culture better and know more about the structure of that society through a study and analysis of the cultures dances. By studying the dances of a particular culture, we gain insight into social relations, rituals and meanings. Dance is an integral part of all cultures that exist in global and local communities (Davida, 2011 Desmond, 1993–1994; Buckland, 2010).

Dance ethnography

The study of cultures requires the methods of an anthropologist. Ethnographic research or field research is the method of choice. Dance ethnography is the study of dance through field research. "Dance Ethnography allows the scholar to venture across diverse populations and cultures. Where a reflexive process takes place in the analysis and writing of the social and cultural practices of the people encountered during fieldwork" (Dankworth & David, 2014, p. 1).

Research strategies for dance and culture

A listing of research strategies for studying dance and culture includes traditional archival research and qualitative research methods including participant observation, direct observation, interviewing (structured and unstructured), case studies, focus groups or narrative accounts.

What to study?

There are a multitude of topics one can study through a cultural lens. For example, one may study the features of a society, rituals and/or meaning expressed through dance.

Features

To learn about the features of a society, researchers study: (a) the steps and the structure of the dances; (b) roles of female and male dancers; (c) the costumes; and (c) the content of the dances.

An example of features of a society comes from a project conducted over many years by Jacquie Malone. Black dance or African American dance forms are representative of a culture and of a time-period. The life of Cholly Atkins, a tap dancer, who became the choreographer for the Motown singing groups is revealed in the book *Class Act: The Jazz Life of Choreographer Cholly Atkins*. Researcher and co-author, Jacqui Malone, drew on many sources including interviews, books, articles, films, panel proceedings, and videos "to create a study of the cultural milieu through which Cholly moved" (Malone & Atkins, 2001, p. xi).

Dance as ritual

The ritual dance allows the inhabitants to celebrate important milestones and events. They are able to express their emotions and channel the hopes and fears through dance. By studying dance as ritual we gain entry into the society from their point of view.

Susan Reed, conducted field research and filmed over 50 hours of video in her research on Sri Lanka dance. "In this book, I explore how a local ritual-based dance form was transformed into an ethnic and national symbol and the consequences this transformation had for the community of traditional dances as well as for new groups of performers especially women" (Reed, 2001, p. 5).

Dance as meaning

Meaning may be expressed through dance in a variety of ways. In some cultures, dance is a way to express and demonstrate power. For example, the gold miners in South Africa performed a gumboot dance that included rhythmic stamping, clapping and chain shaking to communicate to one another in the dark and wet mines—an oppressive environment. Similarly, the Brazilian capoeira was a way to express and demonstrate power through a combination of dance, martial arts and music.

S. Rostas conducted ethnographic research in Mexico to determine the meaning of the Concheros Dance:

> In the field, at least at first, I went to as many dances as possible, staying up for numerous all night vigils (when invited to attend) and listened to, participated in and when appropriate initiated conversations with dancers about the dance. I carried out semi-structured interviews only during the later phases of the project (from 1995 onward) with some of the jefes and dancers ...
>
> *(Rostas, 2009, p. xviii)*

Conclusion

Dance provides a direct view into the life of a people, place and time. Cultures may be studied to gain knowledge of the features, the rituals and the meaning making of a community. By utilizing the tools of the dance ethnographer, the curtain is lifted and reveals the real community.

Sample abstract from the University of Delaware

Separated by cultures, joined by dance

Nick Sisofo

Within each culture are distinct rules, hobbies, and norms that allow each group to stand out from others. One aspect that is universally represented throughout each culture is dance. Through dance, cultures can express what they stand for and what they believe in. As a result, everyone uses dance differently, making it imperative to find the purpose behind each dance. Knowing this, I decided to research cultural similarities and differences of dance in hopes to better the dance community one day. I wanted to see how particular body parts were used to express meaning in each movement. How does each culture compare in their dance movements relative to each body part and the various elements of dance? I worked with the Confucius group, Scottish Country Dance Club, and Delaware Kamaal. Once I had my groups chosen, I did background research on each group to prepare for their performances. Prior to attending each dance group, I also designed a document to help me observe and critique each organization. The document included the background information of each group, the name of the dance, the various elements of dance (space, time, force, relationships), and any additional information. After creating the review sheet, I made sure there were speakers, enough space to dance, and any additional props needed to illustrate the dance. As soon as I had everything, I was ready to watch each group perform their dance piece. From my research, I discovered that dance is universally incorporated into each culture and has a major impact in developing the identity of the culture. In spite of the differences between cultures, they share common movements and themes by their style of dance. To start, the force and time in each dance revolved around the music's tempo. Both the Reel and Va had upbeat and quick music, which led to fast paced, heavy, and sharp movements. Other dances like the Tibetan, Uyghur, and Bharatanatyam had slower music which led to more moderately slow, light, and smoother movements. Another common similarity between each dance was their movements, including their body language, social cues, and facial expressions. Each dance that I looked at had common patterns that expressed dance differently. The Tibetan, Uyghur, and Bharatanatyam incorporated a lot of facial expressions that transcended the overall feeling of the dance. Meanwhile the Va and Reel showed barely any emotions as they were focused more on form. One thing every dance had was organization and basic rules to follow. Whether the dance was free flowing or bound, heavy or light, fast or slow; each required skill and understanding of their bodily movements. In conclusion, each of the cultural dances demonstrated creativity, commitment, compassion, and artistry. Despite each cultures' uniqueness, all of the dances connect individuals and bring people together.

Sample abstracts submitted to NCUR

The primus process: A study of social and cultural connotations in dance

Maya S. Gonzalez, Karl Rogers, Department of Dance, The College at Brockport (SUNY), Brockport, NY 14420

Dr. Pearl Primus (1919–1994), dance anthropologist and a pioneer of modern dance in America, played a significant role in identifying and establishing, for American audiences, African and African-American cultures through dance. This role was manifested through her studies of and immersion in the regional dance cultures of various African countries and of the American South. Her fieldwork resulted in a synthesis of first-hand experiences and research in the form of choreographed works. Within both her anthropological studies and her creative insight, Primus emphasized the importance of process and experiential discovery. This is apparent in her presented works. She recognized the function and purpose behind her artistic works in addition to their presentational value. Through this approach, her works served as commentaries on cultural and personal identity as well as innovative dance pieces. An all-encompassing perspective of Primus's anthropological, creative and intellectual explorations in dance and culture provides fresh insight into these social constructs. Pearl Primus's creative contributions are instituted through a critical study of articles and essays written during various stages of Primus's life, her most recent biography, The Dance Claimed Me, and dance pieces that she created as results of her research. This investigation culminates in a discussion and analysis of Primus's establishment of process over product, her importance to dance history in linking culture and dance, and her means of utilizing dance as a channel for social protest. Through these multiple processes of inquiry, all of which are evident in her choreographed works, Primus showcases her own commentary on the links between culture and dance specifically within African and African-American communities. An extensive consideration of Primus's processes demonstrates that dance is essentially a form of communication, and when utilized to its fullest potential, can express the rawest forms of identity in regard to any individual person, community or culture.

Black dance in America

Brittiney Gardner (Angela Banchero-Kelleher) Department of Dance, Utah Valley University, 800 West University Parkway, Orem, UT 84058

In the 1930s and 40s America was a harsh world full of racial segregation and discrimination. Despite having served in World War II, African Americans were still struggling to gain equal rights and respect from the White Americans. Life in America was segregated and so were many ballet companies. Many black artists resisted the idea that blacks were an inferior race in America. Katherine Dunham was one of those artists who helped the black population to reawaken their artistic roots and take pride in themselves. Katherine Dunham did this through the art of dance. Dunham started her own company where she was able to present black dancers in an acceptable way, so the White Americans would see them as persons. This is reflected in her work "Barrelhouse Blues". As the relations between the separate races started to change in America, due to social/political pressure, dance began to reflect this change as well. The purpose of this research is to demonstrate the ability of dance to reflect the culture. Katherine Dunham's work "Barrelhouse Blues" is a physical reflection of many of the issues confronting African Americans in the 30s and 40s. An analysis of Kathrine Dunham's "Barrelhouse Blues", in 1943, an interview with African, and African American cultural scholars, and research of written works, will yield the answers to the following questions. 1. What were race relations like in American in the 30s and 40s? 2. What were the issues confronting African Americans in the 30s and 40s? 3. How did Dunham's doctoral work inform her philosophy and creative process? 4. How does an analysis of "Barrelhouse Blues" reflect Dunham's philosophy and creative process? 5. How does a synthesis of this information reflect the culture of America in the 30s and 40s?

Anti-American sentiment in the Utah ballroom dance community

Emily Darby, Author, Roger Wiblin, Faculty Mentor, Department of Dance, Utah Valley University, 800 West University Parkway, Orem, Utah 84058

Observations at Utah ballroom dance competitions render a large gap in the participation numbers between the International–style events and American-style events. International events crowd the competition floor while their American counterparts are sparsely populated. This research seeks to find the source of participation disparity in the Utah ballroom population, and to compare Utah statistics to national ballroom dance competition International versus American trends. The results of a survey I conducted of advanced ballroom dance students at Utah Valley University prompted interviews with prominent Utah-based ballroom dance professionals. Further, an analysis of 32 National Dance Council of America (NDCA) competition entries from around the United States in 2010 was undertaken. Readings of the NDCA rulebook, the WDC (World Dance Council) competitive rulebook, authoritative ballroom technique books, and additional print sources also assisted the research process. The results of the research demonstrate underlying negative perceptions towards American styles on the part of Utah ballroom students and instructors. Factual analysis of American and International technique, contrasting Utah and national competition entries, and examination of international competitions and rulebooks demonstrate that this trend is Utah-specific. Interviews with Utah coaches revealed a general lack of training and experience on the part of ballroom professional with American styles. The research indicates that it is this lack of comfort on the part of the professionals that is the source of the negative perceptions in their students. If Utah is to join the rest of the ballroom world, there must be more training and experience in American styles in order to release the stigmas of negativity and to produce dancers of greater versatility to benefit Utah competition numbers.

Asheville salsa: An ethnography of social order in dance

Alexandra H. Griffin, Karin Peterson, Anthropology, University of North Carolina, Asheville, 2500 University Heights, Asheville, NC 28804

Salsa dance was popularized in the Puerto Rican barrios of New York in the 1970s and has since been commercialized and globalized; a hybrid of Latin dance that has been redefined and transformed depending on regional and cultural influence. In Asheville, salsa events tend to draw a Latino/a crowd that does not represent the white-dominated constituency of the city. This ethnography aims to capture the contextual meanings of salsa within the Asheville community, as viewed through the lens of a visibly white, female, middle-class, early-twenties participant-observer. This study followed four locations in which salsa served as a unifying social event that either fostered supportive relationships or served as a social hub. Gender dynamics and class privilege influence the constituency and social ordering in the salsa community, as well as the use of space and time supported by Erving Goffman's concept of spatial brackets. Spatial brackets determine when and where it is appropriate to reevaluate an object of play; in this case the object of play is music and dance. By attending weekly social events to learn salsa and conducting informal interviews with dancers, normative and social expectations were explored within each community. This project explores the nuances and importance of the salsa community in Asheville, taking into account class privilege, white privilege, and accessibility by creating cohesive unified spaces for dancers.

Possible research topics in dance and culture

- Interview males and female dancers to answer the question, Do boys experience dance differently from girls?
- View videos of Phillipine Dance to determine the symbolism revealed through the dance.
- Interview dancers and analyze videos to determine the components of Native American dances in Delaware.
- As a participant-observer, research the types of dances performed by college students at social events.
- Interview international students who are taking a ballroom dance class. Ask them how they perceive the differences between Western ballroom dancing and dances of their culture.
- Study the governmental support of dance in various countries.
- Explore how studying a country's culture can inform the dances that emerge.
- Interview local choreographers regarding the international influences on their choreography.
- Compare the dances of Spain and Greece, by using a movement notation system.
- Explore the connections between international dance and international music.
- Analyze and compare videos of ritual dances performed in Haiti and in Ghana.

Conclusion

Through dance we are able to view the features of a society, the rituals of a culture, and meaning of the movement. As dance ethnographers, students will become immersed in a culture and will gain deep knowledge leading to empathy and a greater sense of the world.

Questions for discussion

1. What is dance? To you? To your social group? To your nation?
2. Describe three methods for collecting data in an ethnographic study
3. What is the role of the participant-observer?

4. Why is studying the dances of a culture important? What do you learn about the culture by studying the dances?
5. What is the relationship between studies of dance history and studies of dance and culture?

References

Buckland, T. J. (2010). Shifting Perspectives on Dance Ethnography. In A. Carter, & J. O'Shea (Eds.), *The Routledge Dance Studies Reader*, 2nd ed. (pp. 335–343). New York: Routledge.

Dankworth, L., & David, A., (2014). *Dance Ethnography and Global Perspective: Identify, Embodiment and Culture*. Basingstoke: Palgrave Macmillan.

Davida, D. (2011). Anthropology at Home in the Art Worlds of Dance. In D. Davida (Ed.), *Fields in Motion. Ethnography in the Worlds of Dance* (pp. 1–16). Canada: Wilfrid Laurier University Press.

Desmond, J. (1993–1994). Embodying Difference: Issues in Dance and Cultural Studies. *Cultural Critique*, 26, 33–63. http://www.jstor.org/stable/1354455

Hanna, J. (1989). The anthropology of dance. In L. Overby, & J. Humphrey (Eds.), *Dance: Current Selected Research Volume 1*(p.219). New York: AMS Press.

Malone, J., & Atkins, C. (2001). Preface and Acknowledgments. In C. Atkins, & J. Malone J. (Eds.), *Class Act: The Jazz Life of Choreographer Cholly Atkins* (pp. ix–xvi). New York: Columbia University Press. Retrieved from http://www.jstor.org.udel.idm.oclc.org/stable/10.7312/atki12364.3

Reed, S. (2001). *Dance and the Nation: Performance, ritual, and politics in Sri Lanka*. Madison: University of Wisconsin Press.

Rostas, S. (2009). Preface and Acknowledgements. In S. Rostas (Ed.), *Carrying the Word: The Concheros Dance in Mexico City* (pp. xv–xxiii). Boulder: University Press of Colorado. Retrieved from http://www.jstor.org.udel.idm.oclc.org/stable/j.ctt46ntnc.5

Research methods

https://course.ccs.neu.edu/is4800sp12/resources/qualmethods.pdf
   https://socialresearchmethods.net/kb/qualmeth.php

15

THE DISCOVERY OF KNOWLEDGE IN DANCE HISTORY

Lynnette Young Overby

> Dancing is a way of knowing the world. History helps us recognize that fact.
> *(Dils & Albright, 2001, p. xiv)*

Summary

Dance history research provides students with an opportunity to explore past dance practices, people and ideas. This chapter provides a brief overview of historical research methods, potential topics to pursue, discussion questions, and sample abstracts. Dance history is a very accessible type of research. Formulating a good question, finding the appropriate primary resources, utilizing analytical skills, and disseminating a coherent essay/performance based on the findings make historical research a popular choice for undergraduate students in dance.

Introduction

Conducting historical research in dance provides the scholar with not only a view into dance through the ages, but also a view into the world, as it existed at the time the dance was performed or created. There are many possibilities for original work in dance history including images, oral histories of dancers, choreographers or audience members, biographies of local or regional companies or choreographers. A particular question guides the interpretation of this data. Dance historians have researched many aspects of dance from a historical view, e.g., the development of modern dance from the 1920s to present day; a specific culture—The History of Black Dance in America—or a particular choreographer from a historical period, e.g., the influence of George Balanchine on Ballet in the 20th century. Undergraduate researchers may focus on one narrow aspect of history for a semester long project.

Step-by-step process of conducting historical research (Busha & Harter, 1980)

1. Recognize a historical problem or identify a need for certain historical knowledge.
2. *Dance example*: beginning in the 1920s, how did Black Dance evolve over time?
3. Gather as much relevant information about the problem or topic as possible.
4. *Dance example*: view choreography that exists on film, interview dancers who performed dances associated with certain time periods.
5. Form a hypothesis that tentatively explains the relationships between historical factors.
6. *Dance example*: Black dance that began as an informal activity became mainstream in subsequent decades.
7. Collect and organization evidence, and then verify the authenticity and strength of the information and its sources.
8. *Dance example*: viewed YouTube videos with examples of dances from each decade, reviewed archived journals, newspaper articles, programs with pertinent information
9. Select, organize, and analyze the most pertinent collected evidence, and draw conclusions
10. *Dance example*: narrowed down focus to social dances of the 1940s–1970s.
11. Record conclusions in a meaningful narrative.
12. *Dance example*: transformed conclusions into a suite of dances with narration.
13. *Dance production*: Suite Blackness: Black Dance in America 1940–1970. Including dances representing various decades.
14. Disseminate findings
15. Live performances, YouTube posting of project, conference presentations and publications.

Primary sources—Essential for historical research

Historians go to primary sources, e.g., diary of George Balanchine or the choreography of Alvin Ailey in the search of evidence to answer questions about what happened in the past and why. When working with primary sources, answering a series of basic questions can help us draw more accurate conclusions.

When trying to gather evidence from a primary source, first try to answer these basic questions. (You may not have enough information to do so.)

1. What is it?
2. Who wrote or made it?
3. When was it written or made?
4. Where was it written or made?

5.   How was it written or made?
6.   What evidence does this source contribute to my research?

Then ask, what is the meaning of this primary source?

1.   Why was this document/object written or made?
2.   Who was the intended audience/user?
3.   What questions does this source raise? What don't we know about this source?
4.   What other information do we have about this document or object?
5.   What other sources are like this one?
6.   What other sources might help answer our questions about this one?
7.   What else do we need to know in order to understand the evidence in this source?
8.   What have others said about this or similar sources?
9.   How does this source help me to answer my research question?
10. How does evidence from this source alter or fit into existing interpretations of the past?

After gathering evidence from primary sources, the undergraduate researcher /historian creates a secondary source by writing about the findings, analyzing them, or putting them together into a story, dance, or other format, reflective of the past.
(Source: http://dohistory.org/on_your_own/toolkit/primarySources.html)

Possible research topics in dance history

- Explore the history of tap dance
- Review the history of dance in Philadelphia in the 20th century
- Describe the Roots and Branches of the Ring Shout
- Interview female dancers of the Judson Dance Theatre
- Review videos and analyze contact Improvisation—from 1970 to the present day
- View videos and describe using a movement notation tool, how Hip Hop evolved from the street to the dance studio
- Using archival data, analyze dance in Sussex County Delaware from an historical perspective
- Using archival data and videos, describe modern dance in 20th century Germany
- Review articles and books on dance imagery to describe the history of dance imagery research
- Describe the types of dances included in 19th century K-12 United States curricula.

- Describe the changes in national standards in dance from the 1994 standards to the existing National Core Arts Standards

Sample abstracts submitted to NCUR

The role of dance in education in the early 20th century and today

Kimie Snapp (Angela Banchero-Kelleher), Department of Dance, Utah Valley State College, Orem, UT 84058, 2008

As America moved into the industrial age the role of children in society changed. This led to a change in the American education system. The theories of John Dewey helped to influence this change in the schools and the thinking of what children should learn. Some of these changes included bringing the arts into public education, including dance. By analyzing the culture at the end of the nineteenth century through the beginning of the 20th century we can learn about what value dance had in education. This can then be compared with the culture of today to help find why these ideals have changed. Today there is a debate in American education of the importance of the arts, music, and dance programs in the schools. By comparing the motivations of educators and the community both today and in the early 20th century we can better understand the current arguments surrounding the benefits of dance in the public school setting. An analysis of books and journal articles exploring the educational theories of John Dewey, the educational climate in the early 20th century, and the role of dance in education will reveal the relationship between dance and education.

From sin to sensation: The progression of dance music from the medieval period through the renaissance

Jillissa Brummel, Dr. Sandra Yang, Music History, Cedarville University, 251 N. Main St., Cedarville, OH, 45314, 2016

This research paper explores how dance music has been part of the foundation for musical art in world history and the key to unlocking information concerning societal atmospheres throughout history. With each age and progression of music came new genres, instruments and social beliefs that were woven through religious and secular culture, each of which impacted the production of dance throughout the centuries. As dance music infiltrated the social and religious scenes of the medieval period, the sacred value of dancing was questioned which is presented through historical sources on pagan culture in the medieval period. Further research on improvements of instrument mechanics in dance music and dance forms are presented through medieval to Renaissance manuscript publications and writings of Guillaume de Machaut, a historically acclaimed figure. Dance forms, instruments, and choreography sought much revision between the two periods, and with the invention of the printing press and common access to publications, drastic innovations in dance culture and music literature were made moving into the Renaissance period. Therefore, the art of music has seen much diversity and change throughout history, causing each individual dance genre to be created and shaped into a product fitting for the time. Because dance music gained historical importance since the medieval period, its rapid progression through oral tradition, religious tradition, and social environments reached new heights in the social and musical life from Medieval times though the Renaissance period.

The history of Axis Dance Company and its correlation within American society and disability rights

Whitney Collins, Faculty Mentor: Angela Banchero-Kelleher, Department: Dance, Institution: Utah Valley University, Institutional Address: 800 W University Pkwy, Orem, UT 84058, 2016

This research sheds light on how the disabled have been discriminated throughout American history. It will guide audiences through laws that have been made to help those with disabilities. In the process of exposing the history of disability rights, this presentation will also shed light on how AXIS Dance Company reflects society's changing views towards those with disabilities through the company's changing movement vocabulary. AXIS Dance Company, founded in 1987, uses physically integrated dance, which is defined as an integration between physically capable dancers and physically impaired dancers. According to their mission statement, AXIS performs contemporary dance routines and educates communities about collaboration between dancers with and without disabilities. Before companies like AXIS were established, disabled individuals were restricted in the ways they could participate in society. In early American history, disabled individuals were hidden, locked up in homes, abused, and fined for their differences. By examining two dances by AXIS, this presentation will yield better understanding towards America's outlook on those with disabilities (from 1900s–2012), and disability rights in America. By critically analyzing the change in movement vocabulary between In This Body and a version of The Narrowing by AXIS Dance Company, from an historical perspective, readers will better understand how AXIS reflects America's cultural views towards those with disabilities (from 1900s–2012). In order to create new knowledge, this research required reading printed source materials, observing videos, and critically analyzing In This Body and a version of The Narrowing. These materials helped answer the following questions: 1. How does historicism (historical frame of analysis) provide more information towards fully understanding historical events? 2. What is the history of disability rights in America? 3. How does a critical analysis of In This Body and a version of The Narrowing yield answers toward understanding the history of disability rights in America?

French society abroad: The popularization of French dance throughout Europe, 1600–1750

Adam Rinehart, Sandra Yang, Department of Music and Worship, Cedarville University, 251 North Main St., Cedarville, Ohio 45314

This paper explores the dissemination of French dance, dance notation, and dance music throughout Europe, and it explains the reasons why French culture had such an influence on other European societies from 1600–1750. First, the paper seeks to prove that King Louis XIV played a significant role in the outpour of French dance and the arts. Next, the paper discusses prominent French writers of dance notation who influenced the spread of French dance literature and training throughout Europe. Finally, the paper delineates European composers and their involvement in the development and production of French dance music. Using academic, peer-reviewed journal articles, books, and other scholarly sources, this paper seeks to accurately present the information in an orderly fashion. The paper contains visual evidence of dance and music notation to assist the reader in understanding the subject matter. Additionally, theories of contemporary authors as well as authors from the time period are discussed to present concrete evidence. The two main types of dance discussed in the paper are ballroom and court dances, which were prominent within the French royal court. One major finding of the research is the fact that French court and ballroom dances were specifically designed to communicate the power and prestige of King Louis XIV; consequently, other European countries were influenced to strive for similar prestige. Another finding is that many forms of French dance notation were translated and published in other countries, which increased the use of French dance throughout Europe. Musically, European composers such as Handel and Mozart included elements of French dance music in their compositions, and thus played a significant role in prevalence of French dance music throughout Europe. Overall, this paper proves that French dance received wide recognition due to political influence, availability of dance notation, and the involvement of prominent composers.

Swinging for change

Cory Baldwin, Angela Banchero, Department of Dance, Utah Valley University, 800 West University Parkway, Orem, UT 84058

The instigation of social change can arise through varied voices. An orator can inspire us to do better. A natural disaster can mobilize people and governments into action. Political revolutions can begin with the people's stomach growling. In New York in the 1920s the catalyst for change was swinging at the Savoy Ballroom. This research will show that the African American dance of the Lindy Hop was the precursor to the great civil rights movement in America. The Savoy ballroom was a mixed establishment, which showed that peaceful racial coexistence was possible. The individuality of the dance form helped to give rise to the voice of Black Americans. The exposure and admiration given to these Black dancers by White audiences helped to boost the national respect all African Americans.

Conclusions

By applying the skills of the historian, the dance student engages the past with a critical eye. The students are also able to devise a variety of communication strategies including, writing, oral presentations and performances. As a historical researcher the student gains background knowledge of a particular topic, individual, place or time.

Discussion questions

1. How is knowledge in dance history created?
2. Does knowledge of dance history or history in general influence performance?
3. Does our perspective change over time?
4. What time period of dance history appeals to you most? Why?

References

Busha, C., & Harter, S. (1980). *Research Methods in Librarianship: Techniques and Interpretations.* New York, NY: Academic Press.

Dils, A., & Cooper Albright, A. C. (2001). *Moving History/Dancing Culture A Dance History Reader.* Middleton, Connecticut: Wesleyan University Press.

16

DANCE SCIENCE

Rachel M. Delauder

If you want to change your body, first change your mind.

(Franklin, 2004)

Summary

This chapter reviews undergraduate research areas of dance science that investigate the physical, mental, and emotional aspects that impact the dancer's body and performance. Examples from recent qualitative and quantitative studies will describe specific benefits of dance science research to dance instructors and students, including enhanced abilities in technique, performance, overall health and well-being. Topics include the evaluation of somatic education, exercise science, and biomechanics. These scientific devices have been shown to incorporate mindful movement, qualitative notation, wellness, training principle methods, physics/biological studies in quantitative movement notation and mechanical data analysis to influence dance training. Undergraduate students are encouraged to explore dance science research from a multidisciplinary approach

Introduction

This chapter will discuss somatic education, exercise science, and biomechanics from a dancer's perspective. It is imperative that the dancer is aware of his or her own body in dance class and performance. Dancers who have a fundamental knowledge of key principles in the dance science disciplines can promote improvements in technique, fitness level, performance quality, and career longevity. Moreover, dance science scholarship is a multidisciplinary study, producing research publications, and thesis focused on physical therapy, athletic training, dance medicine, and kinesiology. Dance science research advances the study of human movement potential, by contributing new knowledge to dance training methods and practices. The benefits of this research include dance safety, minimization to stress on the body, and lowering the risk of injury.

Somatic education

Sensory awareness, imagery, and movement practices

Somatic rooted from the Greek term "soma," meaning the body in its wholeness, encompasses education of body practices in dance techniques that promotes body awareness (Johnson, 2008). Mind-body therapies such as the Alexander Technique, Feldenkrais Method, Bartenieff Fundamentals, Ideokinesis, and the Franklin Method facilitate body exploration, mindfulness, inner physical perception and sensation that strongly differ from the classical performance mechanism. The mind-body therapies methodologies are described as followed: Alexander Technique incorporates phases of conscious control and augmented rest (Cacciatore, Horak, & Henry, 2005). The Feldenkrais Method is a system that uses verbal guided exercises to promote neuromuscular organization between mind and body (Buchanan & Ulrich, 2001). Bartenieff Fundamentals utilize four principles: breath, core support, dynamic alignment, and spatial intent to generate neuro-connections that direct human movement (Feldenkrais, 1981). Sweigard's Ideokinesis utilizes guided visual imagery structured in metaphors improve movement fluidity, alignment and posture (Sweigard, 1974). The Franklin Method uses dynamic neuro-cognitive imagery and anatomical structure to facilitate lasting improvements on mind and body (Wilmerding & Krasnow, 2017).

When somatic education is integrated with science, the technique taught in dance classes, e.g., movement quality, strength, flexibility, and retention are advanced. Somatics provides a physical practice that is either receptive, i.e., somo-emotional release, or active, i.e., investigating sensory awareness that supports an individual's locomotor function (Galeota-Wozny, 2006). The standard practice of body therapies focuses on the dancer utilizing images, imagination, directions, location, and verbal signals/commands to measure his or her, effort, reaction, and sensations occurring within the body. The goal of somatic education is to change habitual movement and positioning during rest and in motion by reducing tension and re-establishing greater control for better alignment, balance, and strength needed for quality dance performance. Somatic education within a dance science curriculum in higher educational programs has the potential to be vital in understanding the impact of sensory awareness (Wilmerding & Krasnow, 2017). Somatic education integrates anatomy, kinesiology, and biomechanics, contact and release methods, with key elements of somatic training such as: "(1) Novel Learning Context, (2) Sensory Attunement, and (3) Augmented Rest" (Green, 2002). The characteristics of somatics is the body learns to apply improvements and generate quality of movement by consciously sensing, initiating, and directing sensory awareness.

Exercise science

Dancers as athletes

Exercise science combined with dance becomes an integrative study of the human body during motion and mechanical function. This multidisciplinary work includes a wide array of modalities designed to assist the dancer in reaching the physiological demands of the body required for optimal performance and career longevity. Exercise science is defined as the study of human movement, health and performance, with a multidisciplinary approach involving biology, physics, anatomy, physiology, kinesiology, biomechanics, body therapies, injuries, rehabilitation, personal health, nutrition, and motorlearning (US National Library of Medicine, 2003). Dance training measures of exercise science include range of motion (ROM), strength, balance, neuromuscular coordination, kinesthetic awareness, and versatility (Zech, Hübscher, Vogt, Banzer, Hänsel, & Pfeifer, 2010); yet, it varies from biomechanics. Biomechanics utilizes exercise science to understand the cause and effect relationship that produces human movement; however, exercise science focuses on human physiology and human function of the anatomy.

Exercise nurtures the dancer's athletic needs by exposing dancers to various levels of intensity and different environmental conditions to enhance skill and performance quality. The best dancers will utilize physical and mental knowledge of exercise science principles for dance artistic expression, technique performance and to produce the desired imagery of choreographers. In addition, this knowledge will provide dancers with the ability to have effective and shorter recovery from injury and rehabilitation (Laws, 2005). Dancers are encouraged to have good cardiovascular fitness, muscular endurance, stamina, muscular strength, power, and flexibility. Exercise science undergraduate programs with dance science course work offer the student access to scientific inquiry and training principles with a dance aesthetic. This knowledge encompasses problem solving and critical thinking of practical applications for dancers to reach their artistic and technical potential. Current research in the area of dance science with an exercise science focus demonstrates the power of this knowledge such as: "Quadriceps strength and jumping efficiency in dancers" (Harley, Gibson, Harley, Lambert, Vaughan, & Noakes, 2002), "Anterior cruciate ligament injuries in female athletes: part two, a meta-analysis of neuromuscular interventions aimed at injury prevention" (Hewett, Ford, & Myer, 2006), and "The shortening reaction of forearm muscles: the influence of central set" (Miscio, Pisano, Del Conte, Pianca, Colombo, & Schieppati, 2001).

Biomechanics

The applications of mechanical and physiological components to dance movement

Have you ever wondered how to achieve greater momentum in jumps, maintain balance in leg extensions, or create faster rotational speed in turns? Dancers utilize their line of gravity, center of mass, and upright posture, which all contribute to the principles of biomechanics. Biomechanical research applies the principles of physics to support growth in execution and artistry. Biomechanics uses physics, biology, mathematics, technology, and engineering applications and analyses to examine the human body's mechanical response during motion and harnesses systematic codes that generate movement (Knudson, 2007). Biomechanics is an integral component of a dancer's function providing tools for fitness and training. This area of study offers rehabilitative methods for dancers to improve dance techniques, prevent disabling injuries, assess fitness level, and control overtraining (Schoene, 2007, p. 3). Biomechanical knowledge also allows dancers to plan dance training and practices. How? Biomechanics is an area of study within dance science that uses technology to capture the intent of movement, internal and external forces, produced behaviors and in response to locomotion, through kinematics. Biomechanics utilizes motion notation, kinematic analysis, kinetic data, computerized cinematography, and movement description of anatomical structure to assess mechanical components such as: ROM, ground reaction forces, gravity, muscular force, velocity, linear and angular kinetics and kinematics, reaction time, etc. This area of dance science examines how components of the body interact during motion as a whole with applied force and degree of workload (Koutedakis, Owolabi, & Apostolos, 2008).

Biomechanical research applies the methodology of movement notation such as motif description and effort-shape description to quantitively detect movement initiation changes in movement functional bodily expression, and use of space, time, and dynamics (Koutedakis, Owolabi, & Apostolos, 2008). Biomechanical and dance science research has been found to be essential in detecting root causes and injury advancement in anatomical imbalances, musculoskeletal deficiency, faulty bone alignment, and injury classification, which has led to a diagnosis and effective rehabilitation methods (Koutedakis, Owolabi, & Apostolos, 2008).

Possible research topics

Somatic education

a   Explore the origins of somatic education and the cultural influences of these dance/movement pioneers:

  • Isadora Duncan, Rudolf von Laban, and Margaret H'Doubler

b   Research 19th-century somatic pioneers:

  • Elsa Gindler and Heinrich Jacoby Gimmler and their discovery of body psychotherapies

c   Implement somatic educational methods and body-work therapies into your dance training practice:

  • Frederick Matthias Alexander (The Alexander Technique), phases of conscious control

- Moshe Feldenkrais (The Feldenkrais Method), verbal guided exercises
- Irmgard Bartenieff (Bartenieff Fundamentals), four principles
- Mabel Todd and Lulu Sweigard (Ideokinesis), visual imagery
- Eric Franklin (Franklin Method), dynamic imagery and anatomical structure
- Body-Mind centering, use of bodily sensation

d   Imagine yourself in a somatic education research program and design your own dance somatic theory-based curriculum

e   Analyze the ways in which somatic educational training is incorporated into learning dance choreography

Exercise science

a   Find out how the energy systems operate with various levels of dance performance intensity

b   Identify specific fitness requirements for optimal dance performance in terms of:

- Aerobic capacity (e.g., endurance activity)
- Anaerobic capacity (e.g., maximal intensity)
- Muscle endurance (e.g., maintaining maximal force)
- Power (e.g., speed component to maximal muscle force)
- Flexibility (e.g., muscle elasticity and ROM)
- Neuromuscular coordination (e.g. balance, agility, coordination, stability, and skill)
- Body composition (e.g., bodily structure)
- Rest (e.g., recovery and regeneration of body)

c   Study the structure and function of the body parts for optimal human movement:

- Primary tissues of the body (e.g., muscle and nerve tissue)
- Body composition and structure (e.g., energy intake and physical activity)
- Bone development and growth (e.g., skeletal muscle and bone structure)
- Body orientation and joint movement (e.g., mobility)
- Cardiovascular system (e.g., stroke volume, heart rate, VO_2 max)

Biomechanics

a   Research the instrumentation used for capturing motion and study the effects of this instrumentation on understanding movement (e.g., motion capture, data processing, and comparative evaluation)

b   Investigate biomechanical research using kinematic software analysis, variables, and technology for human movement transcription

c   Examine motion description and how to apply it to detail body segments:

- Describe basic action and anatomical parts involved
- Direction of movement

- Duration, amount of time
- Transference of weight
- Velocities and acceleration
- Joint angles
- Movement rotation
- Symmetry
- Dynamics
- Angular and relative displacement
- Timing
- Intersegmental coordination

d   Learn how to notate dance movement and techniques:

- Motif description
- Effort-Shape Description
- Structural Description (e.g., body, space, time, and dynamics)

a   Conduct research that builds on past study of mechanical behaviors;

- Gait analysis (e.g., upright posture in motion)
- Postural analysis (e.g., alignment)
- Torque (e.g., external force and body rotation)
- Center of mass (e.g., center of gravity)
- Line of gravity: vertical line running of center of body towards the ground
- Ground reaction force: the forced applied on the body, in relation to the force reaction exerted when in contact with the ground

Sample abstracts submitted from NCUR and the University of Delaware

Changes in alignment during gait after a semester of Franklin Method instruction

Michael Rowley, dance minor capstone, University of Delaware, 2015

The goal of this project was to discern any changes in skeletal alignment during walking after a course in the Franklin Method. Subjects were separated into an experimental group of students training in the Franklin Method (n = 5) and a control group taking another dance course (n = 4). They underwent traditional clinical gait analysis at the beginning and end of the semester. Images were taught from Eric Franklin's *Dynamic Alignment Through Imagery* textbook. Some specific images the experimental subjects reported using during the post-testing included imaging your: central axis as a popsicle stick; central axis as a pole of support from your foot/feet through your head; pelvis as a ball bouncing on your femur heads;

scapulae as sandbags with sand pouring down your back; feet rooted in the ground; and springs under your feet. Spinal alignment was measured as changes in range of motion of three segments around three axes each. The experimental group experienced decreases in range of motion for six of the nine variables. Two of these were statistically significant: head forward tilt and trunk rotation. The control group experienced decreases in three of the nine ranges of motion. Trunk forward tilt showed a significant decrease, and pelvic rotation showed a significant increase. The changes in these spinal alignment variables from pre- to post-tests were also reported. For seven of the variables, the change in the experimental group's range of motion was less than the control group's. The only variable that reached significance at the $p < .05$ level was trunk rotation. Qualitative data were also collected from the experimental group in the form of a survey. Answers for how they perceived their gait to be different included: felt lighter on their feet; felt less pounding with each step; more stability in the supporting foot; and more lifted while walking. Participants reported that the central axis images and the pelvis-as-a-ball image were the most useful. All of the data acquired in this experiment point toward a positive effect of imagery training and usage on gait.

Supplemental training of dancers

Chelsea Salcido (Jason V. Slack) (Amy Markgraf-Jacobson), Department of Physical Education and Recreation, Utah State University, 2009

The dancers of the world today are expected to perform physically demanding skills. The physical performance between what is done in dance classes rehearsals and on-stage performances are all physically different. With the time constraints on collegiate dancers the supplemental training that needs to take place rarely occurs. Purpose: To determine if using part of the technique class time to train the more athletic side of dance and can bridge the gap between the physical demands of dance class, rehearsal and on-stage performance. Methods: 23 female dancers enrolled in a 5 day a week, hour and twenty-minute, level one collegiate modern technique class participated in a supplemental conditioning program within the class time allotted. Two of the 5 days in class were focused to a circuit training program. The other 3 out of the 5 days were focused to the technical aspects of modern dance. As a control another level one collegiate modern technique class participated focusing just on the technical aspects of modern dance 5 days a week. Results: The data was analyzed using a T-test to determine that the control and the exercise group did not differ in age, gender, years dancing and several other demographical variables. We will use a dependent T-test to determine the pre-post differences. Conclusion: As our research concludes we hope to suggest cardiovascular exercise and dance specific muscle strength exercises should be added to the traditional technique classes. This supplemental dance specific training should be done during class time and not during dancers own time.

How we move: An integration of dance and biological science

Liza Bustle and Susie Thiel, Department of Theatre, University of Kentucky

The sciences and arts are historically polarizing fields that intersect at the point of creativity. According to Smith (1959) "Creation excites creation: perceptive poetry stimulates the scientist, and a keen scientific insight into nature stimulates the poet." The goal of this research study is to further explore the collaborative products resulting from this amalgamation of science and art, particularly in the biological and dance realms. In doing so, the analytical processes of the two areas will be compared, showing the difference in the mindset that accompanies the creative processes associated with each field. For example, the question, "How do we move?" can be answered through these two differing perspectives. Anatomically we move by the sliding of actin and myosin filaments in muscle myofibrils; however, dancers could depict movement as curving pathways with reaching arms and varying focus. The research methods for this study included the reading of publications on creativity, choreography, and cross-disciplinary material. Live performances and performance videos from various choreographers' archives were examined for choreographic material, use of multi-media, text, and audience interaction. Scientific discoveries were also analyzed for artistic content. While there were no examples found directly relating to dance, there were multiple discoveries that originated with creative thinking. The results of the study identified multiple choreographers and organizations that specialize in the fusing of biology into dance in order to educate through concept visualization and kinesthetic learning. The methodical characteristics of science inspired sections of the examined choreography as well, incorporating structural foundations within the pieces. Additional pieces were found with commentary on controversial ethics relating to the biological field. This intersection between biology and dance has impacted society by breaking the traditional molds of how scientists and artists should function. The crossing of the two fields has enlightened colleagues in each discipline, providing knowledge and insight from different perspectives. This connection between the two fields unites the mind, body, and movement while allowing the opposing disciplines to coexist harmoniously, fueling creation in each area.

Conclusion

Dance science is a vast growing multidisciplinary field in biokinesiology, physical therapy and applied physiology programs, and has become popular among dance majors. This chapter provided introductory information in the areas of somatics, exercise science and biomechanics. Dance science research and application supports the development of teaching approaches that will benefit dancers in technique classes, in performance and those who are returning from a musculoskeletal injury. Dance medicine is needed for more educational and research advancements to improve a dancer's health in training and performance. Go ahead, support your passion for two worlds, and dive into dance scientific research now!

Questions for discussion

1. How do physical, mental and emotional aspects of dancing influence each other?
2. What are the similarities and differences between the Alexander Technique, Bartenieff Fundamentals, and Feldenkrais Method?
3. How are the components of exercise science that are different from biomechanics?
4. What projects can be co-authored with science majors?
5. What science disciplines are most connected with dance?
6. Why is biomechanics important to the dance researcher?
7. How do biomechanical quantitative analysis and clinical assessment serve for dance purposes?

Reference

Buchanan, P. A., & Ulrich, L., (2001). The Feldenkrais Method: A dynamic approach to changing motor behavior. *Res. Q. Exer. Sport.*, 72, 315–323.

Cacciatore, T. W., Horak, F. B., & Henry, S. M. (2005). Improvement in Automatic Postural Coordination Following Alexander Technique Lessons in a Person with Low Back Pain. *Physical Therapy*, 85(6), 565–578.

Franklin, E. (2004). *Conditioning for Dance*. Champaign IL: Human Kinetics.

Feldenkrais, M., (1981). *The Elusive Obvious*. Cupertino, CA: Meta Publications.

Galeota-Wozny, N. (2006). Somatics 101. *Dance Magazine*, July.

Green, J. (2002). Somatic Knowledge: The Body as Content and Methodology in Dance Education. *Journal of Dance Education*, 2(4), 114–118.

Harley, Y. X., Gibson, A. S. C., Harley, E. H., Lambert, M. I., Vaughan, C. L., & Noakes, T. D. (2002). Quadriceps strength and jumping efficiency in dancers. *J. Dance Med. Sci.*, 6 (3), 87–94.

Hewett, T. E., Ford, K. R., & Myer, G. D. (2006). Anterior cruciate ligament injuries in female athletes: Part two, a meta-analysis of neuromuscular interventions aimed at injury prevention. *Am. J. Sports. Med.*, 34(3), 490–498.

Johnson, D. H. (2008). *The Body in Psychotherapy: Inquires in Somatic Psychology*. Retrieved November, 23, 2008 from http://www.donhanlonjohnson.com

Koutedakis, Y., Owolabi, E. O., & Apostolos, M. (2008). Dance Biomechanics: A Tool for Controlling Health, Fitness, and Training. *Journal of Dance Medicine & Science*, 12(3), 83–90.

Knudson, D. V. (2007). Introduction to biomechanics of Human movement. In D. V. Knudson, *Fundamentals of biomechanics* (2nd ed.) (pp. 3–22). New York, NY: Springer. Retrieved from http://www.profedf.ufpr.br/rodackibiomecanica_arquivos/Books/Duane %20Knudson-%20Fundamentals%20of%20Biomechanics%202ed.pdf

Laws, H. (2005). *Fit to Dance 2: Report of the Second National Inquiry into Dancers' Health and Injury in the UK*. London: Dance UK.

Miscio, G., Pisano, F., Del Conte, C., Pianca, D., Colombo, R., & Schieppati, M. (2001). The shortening reaction of forearm muscles: the influence of central set. *Clin. Neurophysiology*, 112, 884–894.

Schoene, L. M. (2007). Biomechanical evaluation of dancers and assessment of their risk of injury. *J. Am. Podiatr. Med. Assoc.*, 97(1), 75–80.

Sweigard, L. (1974). *Human Movement Potential: Its Ideokinetic Facilitation*. New York: Dodd-Mead.

US National Library of Medicine. (2003). *Exercise Science. Collection Development Manual*. Retrieved from https://www.nlm.nih.gov/tsd/acquisitions/cdm/subjects34.html

Wilmerding, M. V., & Krasnow, D. H. (2017). Mental Training. In M. V. Wilmerding, & D. H. Krasnow (Eds.), *Dance Wellness* (pp. 58–68). Champaign IL: Human Kinetics and IADMS.

Zech, A., Hübscher, M., Vogt, L., Banzer, W., Hänsel, F., & Pfeifer, K. (2010). Balance Training for Neuromuscular Control and Performance Enhancement: A Systematic Review. *Journal of Athletic Training*, 45(4), 392–403. http://doi.org/10.4085/1062-6050-45.4.392

17

PSYCHOLOGICAL AND COGNITIVE ASPECTS OF DANCE

Lynnette Young Overby

bodily movement is essential to an understanding of all aspects of life

(Warburton, 2011)

Summary

The mental aspects of dance provide a rich area of research. Along with traditional text and questionnaire-based instrumentation, new techniques and understanding from brain sciences enable us to observe changes in the brain that occur at the moment one is dancing or while imagining dancing. We can also observe changes that may occur as a result of dance experiences. In this chapter, imagery, embodied cognition, and creativity will be introduced as examples of psychological and cognitive aspects of dance.

Introduction

The mental aspects of dance are equally as important as the physical aspects of dance. Research in this area may include both qualitative and quantitative methodologies.

Many of the methods involved in studying cognitive aspects of dance derive from work in sub-disciplines of psychology including sport psychology and cognitive psychology (Taylor & Taylor, 1995; Taylor & Estanol, 2015). Recently neuroscientists have begun to study dance and dancers. In this chapter, we will consider some of the research that encompasses areas relating to mind—body connections. There will be a specific focus on imagery, creativity and embodied cognition.

Movement imagery

As a student of dance, you have probably experienced a teacher or director using some type of imagery to enhance your performance. For example, to enhance the flow of a movement sequence, a teacher may have you imagine moving as if you are moving through water, or jump by imagining springs on the bottom of your feet.

Dance imagery is the deliberate use of the senses to mentally rehearse a particular skill or sequence in the absence of or in combination with overt, physical movement. The images may be real or metaphorical movements, objects, events, or processes (Overby & Dunn, 2011). Dance imagery research has been conducted to better understand imagery use by dancers and dance teachers, imagery ability, and imagery interventions (Overby, Hall, & Haslem, 1998; Nordin & Cumming, 2005).

The work of Allen Paivio provided a theoretical perspective for some of the imagery research including dance imagery (Paivio, 1985). His dual-coding theory posits that imagery may be visual or verbal. Craig Hall, a colleague of Paivio in the area of kinesiology, expanded on this notion by introducing visual and kinesthetic aspects of imagery. Intervention studies have also demonstrated the impact of imagery strategies on technique and performance. Andrea Bianculli, an undergraduate dance minor and neuroscience major who graduated from the University of Delaware in 2013, conducted an intervention study using the Franklin Method. Her abstract appears in the abstract section of this chapter.

Embodied cognition

What is embodied cognition?

Embodied cognition is a multidisciplinary research area that encompasses both memory and self-understanding because it is the body in motion that enables us to gain knowledge about the art form, about other disciplines and about ourselves. It is defined as the existence of a memory system that encodes knowledge of a person's physical competencies (Grafton, 2009, p. 97)

Recently, neuroscientists have discovered that dance can be an important activity in revealing brain-based information. Sevdalis and Keller state, "Dance has the potential to be not only beautiful in the aesthetic sense but also bountiful in what it reveals about cognition, action, and human interaction" (Sevdalis & Keller, 2011, p. 97).

An example is demonstrated in creative dance. A recent EEG research study revealed the effects on the brain while imagining a performing of a waltz step, and while imagining performing an improvised dance—with higher creative demands. More pronounced alpha activity in the frontal, frontal temporal, and centro temporal brain regions occurred during the creative dance imagery (Fink, Graif, & Neubauer, 2009).

Warburton's research takes us a step further in our understanding of cognition and dance by proposing the topic of dance enaction. This term was based on extensive research and his explorations of marking as a little researched strategy used by dancers to recall choreography (Warburton, 2011; Warburton, Wilson, Lynch, & Cuykendall, 2013).

Students who are studying cognitive science in addition to their dance training will find this a fascinating area to explore.

Creativity

Dance is a creative art form. Historically, the construct of creativity was studied and measured by psychologists through the use of laboratory tests and questionnaires (Witkin, 1962). Brennan (1989) applied this paradigm to dancers in a series of studies; however, she also developed more dance specific measures. Recent research with performing artists including dancers have provided neuro-scientists with real world opportunities to research both the creative process and product (Gruzelier, 2014). The methodology has included EEG-neurofeedback mechanisms, Alpha/Theta (AT) sensory-motor rhythm (SMR) and heart rate variability (HRV) protocols. Creativity research has contributed to our understanding of the role of experience in the arts on creative behavior.

Conclusions

Cognitive aspects of dance including movement imagery, creativity, and embodied cognition provide much potential for the multidisciplinary study of dance. Collaborations with cognitive science research professors and sport psychologists may prove to be a fruitful area of discovery for you.

Possible topics for research

- Survey teachers to determine the types of images dance teachers use in the studio.
- Utilize a movement observation tool to determine whether or not kinesthetic imagery is more effective than visual imagery as a teaching tool.
- Provide dancers who are preparing for a performance with a standardized anxiety instrument to determine their level of anxiety before a performance.
- Determine the effect of a guided imagery intervention (designed to reduce anxiety) on movement by analyzing dancers' performance before and after a concert.
- Compare the imagery used by dance teachers with imagery used by gymnastic coaches.
- Review the literature on embodied cognition by philosophers, psychologists and dance scholars.
- Review the past scholarship on creativity conducted by psychologists and dance scholars.
- Collaborate with a student in neuro-science to design a study that assesses and compares the cognitive processes of dancers and non-dancers.
- Explore differences in levels of creative thinking of dancers, musicians and visual artists.
- Compare the creativity scholarship conducted by dance scholar Mary Alice Brennan with the current work of dance scholar Ted Warburton.

University of Delaware abstracts

Embodied cognition & dance: Does stimulating motor movement impact the results of a thinking task?

Melissa Brower, neuroscience major and dance minor, dance capstone, University of Delaware, 2018

Have you ever wondered about the relationship between the brain and the body? Are you curious if motor movement can enhance one's ability to think more accurately? These are the kinds of topics I initially questioned, which sparked my interest for this project. Because my major is cognitive science, I decided to hone in on the topic of embodied cognition and how it can be applied to dance. According to Fischer & Coello (2015), embodied cognition postulates that our conceptual knowledge is intertwined with our sensory and motor aspects. In other words, there is a predicted relationship between the mind and the physical body. For my project, I performed an experiment to prove a positive relationship between these two entities. To perform my experiment, I gathered a group of 6 dancers, all at the same college level of dance experience, and I divided them evenly into a control and an experimental group. Both of these groups watched a 30 second video on my computer, of myself performing a routine. Following this, they each individually answered a series of 10 simple questions related to the routine, which they had just seen. However, the difference being, the experimental group had actually learned and performed the routine before answering these questions, whereas the control group did not. I hypothesized that the experimental group would perform better on the questionnaire because they would be stimulating their muscles and truly conceptualizing about the routine. The procedures included both groups watching a video of a choreographed dance. The experimental group answered 90% of the questions correctly and the control group answered 60–70% correctly. This project portrayed not only the quantitative results of this mind/body relationship, but also the importance behind the recognition of this relationship for dancers. Dancers use their emotions & personalities to perform, which is why being able to fully immerse oneself in the material is so important. I hope to continue to promote this message to dancers and encourage them to dance outside of their comfort zones.

The Franklin Method applied to improving dance technique

Andrea Bianculli, neuroscience major and dance minor, dance minor capstone, 2013

For my dance minor capstone project, I conducted research on the Franklin Method and its application in improving dance technique. The Franklin Method activates mind and body function through the use of imagery, experiential anatomy, and reconditioning movement to improve function. It capitalizes on the plasticity of the brain, or the brains ability to reorganize neural pathways as a result of new experiences. As a Neuroscience and Biology double major, I was very interested in how the brain can be used to modify the ways in which we move our bodies. Since I'm a dancer always looking to improve technique, I was interested in learning how effective the Franklin Method could be in doing just that. I recruited 5 college –aged female dancers who had no experience with the Franklin Method. They learned choreography that consisted of four cts of eight and included a pirouette, a grand jete, a chaine turn and arabesque. Measurements were based on the height of the grand jete, the height of the back leg in an arabesque, the time dancer could balance after completing the pirouette turn and the alignment of body after completing the chaine turn. Specific Franklin images were given to the dancers over a course of 5 weeks. Throughout the course of the project, video recording was used each week to record the results and allow for data analysis. I also took individual pictures of the dancers performing each aspect of technique before and after the images were given to allow for analysis in greater detail. The results of the study confirmed my belief that the Franklin Method would improve dances technique. The dancers improved in all their performance of the pirouette, grand jete, chaine turn and arabesque. All participants stated that they could foresee themselves utilizing Franklin imagery in the future to improve aspects of their technique that they often struggle with.

Sample abstracts submitted to NCUR

The pursuit of acceptance: A creative process in dance

Katie Erdman (Victoria Hutchinson), Department of Communication Arts, Salisbury University, Salisbury, MD 21801

This presentation will summarize eight stages in the creative process of The Pursuit of Acceptance, a modern dance that was choreographed and presented in the fall of 2007 at Salisbury (Maryland) University. The goal of the creative process was to push past personal boundaries and choreograph a more meaningful and unique piece than any other work I have previously set. The dance was inspired by the death of my grandmother and the difficulty my family had in accepting the loss. The dance, a tribute to her, is about the pursuit of acceptance through stages of grief (shock, anger, denial, bargaining, depression, and acceptance) and the journey of coming to terms with loss. There will be eight stages of the creative process will be examined and summarized in the presentation: the first, is getting started (idea for the dance, choreography proposal and audition, casting audition); second, is the choreography (developing the movement, gesture motifs, sections of the dance, use of props and symbolism); third, are the studio rehearsals; the fourth stage are the production tasks (press release, program text); fifth, are the theatrical elements (music, costumes, lighting); the sixth stage is the technical and dress rehearsals; seventh is the performance; and the eighth stage is my reflection. The presentation will be highlighted by studio and performance photographs, selections of music, and a DVD showing of the 5-minute work. The presentation will conclude with questions and answers.

In between: Research of creative processes

Andrea N. Montez (Dr. Maura Keefe), Department of Dance, The College at Brockport, State University of New York, Brockport, NY 14420

At the start of the semester in Beginning Composition, the first assignment was to simply make a phrase. There were no guidelines to follow; the class merely had to contemplate generating movement. In the case of the phrase that is subject of this presentation, the central theme was discovering material challenging to execute while moving through space, with emphasis on upward direction of focus. Unexpectedly, this brief movement phrase would become the "core" of the final piece entitled In Between. Looking back at the "process" to compose the dance no "process" is recalled at all. This allowed the question to arise: Did a "choreographic process" occur without acknowledgement? If so, what defined the "process?" This presentation first shows the final piece of choreography and then raises a series of discussion points regarding the creative process. In order to make sense of the personal questions about the process the book Dance Composition: A Practical Guide to Creative Success in Dance Making (Jacqueline M. Smith-Autard) was used as a framework alongside physical movement research. Smith-Autard explains, the "composition of a successful dance pre-supposes that the composer has knowledge of the material elements of dance, methods of construction; which gives a form to a dance, and an understanding of the style in which the composer is working." She also explains, composing a dance "involves putting your imagination to work to make something new, to come up with new solutions to problems." Placing my reading of Dance Composition in practice I argue that dance composition relies on the choreographer's previous knowledge of dance, while relying on the involvement of imagination in addition to innovative ways of creating "solutions for problems."

Body image and eating disorders in the world of ballet

Lindsey A. Gasper, Dr. Mark Aune, University Honors Program, California University of Pennsylvania, 250 University Avenue, California, PA 15419

In the world of preforming arts, particularly the field of Ballet, the pressure to look no less than perfect is always on. As someone who danced for 14 years, my typical outfit for class included tight-fitting leotards and tights, which exposed the truest shape of my body. My hair was pulled into a bun and slicked back completely off of my face, leaving nothing to conceal any of my facial features. Every time I had class I was expected to dress this way, and "look like a dancer," regardless of the fact that I did not dance at a professional ballet school. However, this same attire is also worn by the most skillful of dancers who audition with the hopes of being accepted into the top ballet schools in the nation and eventually performing professionally. The auditions the striving performers go to occur in front of critics, some of which are there specifically to look at and judge the dancer's body and appearance. These and many other factors make the dancing community a perfect target for body image and eating disorders. The disorders range from the more commonly heard of anorexia and bulimia, to the less common body dysmorphic disorder. In my Ballet Technique I course at California University of Pennsylvania, we discussed the prevalence of these disorders in dancers. As a supplement to the course, I researched the most common eating disorders and body image disorders among dancers. Using literature pertaining to the subject, I was able to discuss, compare, and contrast the disorders, the main causes of them in dancers, and how they affect the world of performing arts. My poster includes statistics on the several disorders I have researched such as the signs of each disorder, the percentage of dancers who have had or currently have the disorder, and treatment options. The number of dancers with a body image or eating disorder is significantly higher than the number of those being treated for one. This shows that battling a disorder dealing with an individual's appearance rises to a whole new level in the intense world of ballet.

Conclusions

Movement imagery, embodied cognition, and creativity are three examples of the many aspects of psychological and cognitive aspects of dance. Through both qualitative and quantitative explorations, many questions regarding the mind-body relationship may be explored. The answers to these questions will promote a more holistic approach to dance education and performance.

References

General

Taylor, J., & Estanol, E. (2015). *Dance Psychology for Artistic and Performance Excellence*. Champaign, IL: Human Kinetics

Taylor, J., & Taylor, C. (1995). *Psychology of dance*. Champaign, IL: Human Kinetics.

Movement imagery

Nordin, S., & Cumming, J. (2005). Professional dancers describe their imagery: Where, what, why and how. *Sport Psychologist*, 19, 395–416.

Overby, L., & Dunn, J. (2011). The history of dance imagery: Implications for teachers. *IADMS Bulletin for Teachers*, 3(2), 9–11.

OverbyL., Hall, C., & Haslem, I. (1998). A comparison of imagery used by dance teachers, figure skating coaches, and soccer coaches. *Imagination Cognition Personality*, 17(4), 323–337.

Paivio, A. (1985). Cognitive and motivational functions of imagery in human performance. *Can J Appl Sport Sci*, 10, 22–28.

Embodied cognition

Fink, A., Graif, B., & Neubauer, A. C. (2009). Brain correlates underlying creative thinking: EEG alpha activity in professional versus novice dancers. *Neuroimage*, 46, 854–862.

Grafton, S. (2009). Embodied cognition and the simulation of action to understand others. *The Year in Cognitive Neuroscience 2009 Ann. New York Academy of Sciences*, 1156, 97–117.

Sevdalis, V., & Keller, P. (2011). Captured by motion: Dance, action understanding, and social cognition. *Brain and Cognition*, 77, 231–236. doi:10.1016/j.bandc.2011.08.005

Warburton, E. C. (2011). Of meanings and movements: Re:languaging embodiment in dance phenomenology and cognition. *Dance Research Journal*, 43(2), 65–83.

Warbuton, E. C., Wilson, M., Lynch, M., & Cuykendall, S. (2013). The cognitive benefits of movement reduction: Evidence form dance marking. *Psychological Science*, 24(9), 1732–1739.

Creativity

Brennan, M. (1989) The relationship between creative ability in dance style, and creative attributes. In L. Overby, & J. Humphrey (Eds.), *Dance Current Selected Research Volume 1* (pp.1–10). New York: AMS Press.

Gruzelier, J. (2014). EEG—Neurofeedback for optimizing performance. II: Creativity, the performing arts and ecological validity. *Neuroscience and Bio Behavioral Reviews*, 44, 142–158.

Witkin, H. (1962). *Psychological differentiation*. New York: Wiley.

18

APPLICATION AND ACTIVATION

Choreography interacting with digital media

Mary Lynn Babcock

> The two mediums (dance and technology) can be mixed, blended, separated, and deconstructed not only in performance but also in the choreographic process.
>
> *(Babcock, 2018)*

Summary

Interweaving choreography with digital media is exciting for students to learn about and explore. At the undergraduate level, a dance and technology course serves as an introductory survey of choreographic integrations with digital media and 2-dimensional design theory all leading up to the theory and application of interactive media in choreography using Isadora® Interactive software. This chapter on dance and technology describes student involvement with interactive media in the choreographic and performance process by including suggested topics, conclusion, and discussion questions.

Introduction

This chapter is about research on integrating choreography with digital media. It is actually a process of 'interweaving' the two together. Commonly called dance and technology or dance and media, this work is exciting for students to learn about and explore. I use the term "interweaving" because the two mediums can be mixed, blended, separated, and deconstructed not only in performance, but also in the choreographic process. At the undergraduate level, a dance and technology course offered at the University of North Texas serves as an introductory survey of choreographic integrations with digital media and 2-dimensional design theory, all leading up to the theory and application of interactive media in choreography using Isadora® Interactive software. The dance technology information incorporated in this course is the focus of this chapter, which includes examples of interactive media and the performance process through choreographic research. Outcomes, discussion questions, and examples of work by the author and students are included.

Defining the work

The dance technology course is designed to provide dance majors with skills and techniques that will prepare them in multimedia use as it relates to dance creation, education, production, and research. The goal is to provide students with a foundation in the use of digital media and associated software applications that they can directly apply to the field of dance, and more specifically to choreography. Based on the theories of design and composition in video shooting and editing, photography, sound editing, and choreography, students will be able to do the following each project:

- Work with digital media: interactive-real-time processing software and cameras
- Learn how to use the software application, Isadora® to provide interactive control over
- digital media and share work with the class
- Choreograph and perform short studies, and a multimedia informal showing that integrates digital media

Conclusions/outcomes

An overarching learning outcome is in the way this work extends dance literacy through multiple facets. Students learn to use the interplay between the choreographic process, 2-dimensional design theory[1], and the language of software application as it relates to their dance-making. Investigating the integration of digital media within the choreographic and performing process deepens learning because students are actively engaging in multi-modal languages of choreography, software, program design, and live-real time processing. This is not an easy feat to accomplish! For many dance majors, this is the first time they have worked with digital media in relationship with choreography, so they are learning not only how to use the media and the associated software to develop their craft, but they are also learning the artistry of the craft as well.

In the long-term investigation, students develop self-knowledge through their moving and through their programing by investigating how the two interweave and intersect. When working with digital media, students begin looking at their work more objectively as more meaningful art work with less ego, or that the ego transcends into an idea to be explored.

In order to develop an artistic eye for shooting and editing, the students in the dance technology course learn the theory and application of 2-dimensional design aspects (Levin, cited in Babcock, 2018). This all sounds complex as the learning curve is steep. But in its most basic inquiry these students are gaining hands-on tools for investigating and exploring the relationships between the live body and the virtual image through choreography, digital media design, and performance.

In all, this work has led the students to discover and learn about dance through the use of technology. This knowledge is reflected in their student projects and clarity in articulating what they found significant in the process. This work impacts student learning because it engages the students to find meaning in their notions of self within the media that also connects and integrates with their choreography. They come to the understanding of 'who they are' inside the movement, and how that translates to media. Students learn that this relationship is dialectic, and that a successful interaction is one that clarifies when and how the two mediums intersect. In addition, they find the use of symbols which takes them directly into popular culture, society, and the media, which insists by its very nature to support explorations of community issues, individual concerns, cultural tensions, and/or contemporary problems. While symbols and associated cultural connections are not part of this chapter, it is certainly a worthy project to investigate.

Within the integration of the media, the choreography and performance learning occurs on a much deeper level than before because students become active participants in their own learning and outcomes.

Babcock explains:

> This hands-on approach coupled with using 2-dimensional design theory gives [students] them direct tools in finding and utilizing more clear intersections. They develop self- knowledge through their moving and connecting to the media. Practice transforms students' relationship with their tendency to "other" their bodies, because of this practice. Through exploring intent through various activities that cultivate intuition, awareness of bodily emotion, kinesthetic awareness, and corporeal imagination, all of which are grounded in a somatic practice, in which bodies are agents in power relations, rather than experiencing self as mere objects. Empowering, empowered, EMBODIED self is what is significant about this work.
>
> *(Babcock, 2018)*

Students gained confidence in their work as artists because they began looking at how to connect with the image or the other, which interestingly is part of their own process. They begin to find the power in choreographic intent and how media can support and build on it in their work. They begin to make choices based on the tools of the craft combined with their artistic eye. An example of this type of learning comes from a student's self-analysis. McCartney states:

I've loved figuring out how to make the video and live movement become one this semester. It has shown me that there's more to dance other than physical movement but using the elements and video stills and soft movements really makes it come full circle, showing me how they can relate to each other. Looking for the negative space in the video and how you can make that a positive space with the live performer and vice versa. It has really helped me expand my creativity and has made me think outside of the usual dance box.

(McCartney, 2017)

The following excerpt from a student assessment in 2016 indicates how technology advanced how this student sees dance. She points out the strengths and where she would edit so that she could better frame what she refers to as the entire picture. The link to the video excerpt of this project entitled Scar-let Memories is found below. Taylor-Hughlett states:

I learned that technology can be integrated into dance to tell a story and invite audience members to experience that story more personally. This is important because our world is changing and progressing digitally and as artists we have to find creative, innovative ways to use technology to keep the art of dance alive, and interesting. Art doesn't have to be a cookie cutter version of what has been done in the past but by using what has already been done and integrating new methods into our field we expand our not only our own minds to the power of the possibilities in dance, but we challenge and expand the minds of our audiences. I am proud of the work that we have accomplished, and I can see this work being extended and further developed for future projects. If there was something that I could change I would choreograph the piece as a solo on someone else to help me see the entire picture.

(Taylor-Hughlett, 2016)

Where are we today? As performance and technology modalities can quickly morph into newer realms of cyber-culture, discussions emerge around polarity issues of the virtual body vs. the real, space vs. live space and, as some point out, has created an entirely new "ambiguous zone" that is an alternate mode of analyzing the fusion between the dancing body and technology (Santana & Iazetta, 2005). Blurring these lines with the presence of dancers, interactions with sound and images during performance, and interactions with the audience are entirely possible now. Live streaming performances and social media are also integral to today's learners.

Providing this work gives them opportunity to expand their notions of what dance is. In the process, they learn from each other. As Chvasta states in her work, "... we also learn from our students who increasingly perceive digital technology as an integral component of everyday life and art" (Chvasta, 2005, p 157). In all, teaching and learning to interweave digital media and choreography moves processing into new levels of experiences whereby the body can be experienced as the virtual, and space has infinite possibilities.

Research questions framing ways to investigate work with the live and virtual body:

- When/how is the live body seen? When and how is the virtual body seen? How/where do the virtual and live intercept? Investigate how the answers to these questions support choreographic ideas.
- While moving to an image, consider relationships, shapes, and actions that are parallel to the image or in direct contrast. Moving from one scene to the next provides powerful possibilities in actual moving transitions.
- Identify how to use the media[2] that will support the choreographic intent. For example, if one is interested in working with the intent of moving into and out of spaces, then using the media as a lighting source expands the performative space to include a virtual playing field that is filled with possibilities. See Figures 18.1–18.4.
- Review current research/choreographic practices that utilize technology in dance performances.

Sample of Satellite-Dance Company and dance technology projects

Title: **Shade *(2013). Projected images and screen color interact change as the dancers move***

Title: **i.e. creases *(2015). Student course project using Isadora®***

Title: **i.e. Scar-Let Memories *(2016). Student course project using Isadora®***

These students worked primarily with saturated color/intensity. https://www.you tube.com/watch?v=RPSLtRix_2I

Conclusion

This chapter on dance technology is based on a course taught to undergraduate dance majors at North Texas University. Students gain knowledge and skills in dance and technology through the process of 'interweaving' because the two mediums can be mixed, blended, separated, and deconstructed not only in performance, but also in the choreographic process. Undergraduate dance scholars may use an embodied research approach to explore and create new choreography with a technology blend.

Questions for discussion

1. What is dance technology?
2. How can embodied research in dance technology lead to new understanding?

FIGURE 18.1 *Shade* (2013)
Choreography: Mary Lynn Babcock with choreographic contributions from the cast. Photo credit: Milton Adams. Artistic Director: Satellite-Dance Collective; choreographic contributions from the cast. Projection Designer: Scott Martin. Cast: Kihyoung Choi, Cassie Farzan Panah, Amiti Perry, Taryn Tompkins. Costumes: Amiti Perry. Shade is the place of shelter unraveled through broken lines and arrhythmic gestures fighting for balance through counterbalance. An afterthought, a memory, a deep knowing that the edge of another side is home…inside….

FIGURE 18.2 *Shade* (2013)
Choreography: Mary Lynn Babcock with choreographic contributions from the cast. Photo credit: Milton Adams.

FIGURE 18.3 *Shade* (2013)
Choreography: Mary Lynn Babcock with choreographic contributions from the cast.
Photo credit: Milton Adams.

FIGURE 18.4 *i.e. creases* (2015)
The working metaphor for this project became into and out of small spaces. Lighting
and transitions were the primary focus. Photo credit: Mary Lynn Babcock.

3. What technological tools can be used in dance?
4. Do you think dance technology should be a part of every dance student's education? Why or why not?

Notes

1 2-dimensional design aspects found in line, form, color, texture, rhythm, perspective are just a few aspects.
2 Choices on how to use the image as environment, character, lighting source, or cinema add clarity to the project (Troika Ranch iWorkshop, summer 2007).

References

Babcock, M. L. (2018). From here to here: Teaching interactions between the live and virtual self in choreography. In L. Overby, & B. Lepczyk (Eds), *Dance: Current Selected Research Volume 9* (pp. 239–260). Newark, DE: University of Delaware on-line publications.
Chvasta, M. (2005). Remembering Praxis: Performance in the digital Age. *Text and Performance Quarterly*, 25(2), 156–170.
McCartney, S. (2017). Student Self-Assessment—section 3 Learning outcomes, Fall 2017.
Santana, I., & Iazetta, F. (2005). Ambiguous Zones, the intertwining of dance and world in the technological era. Retrieved from http://www.digitalcultures.org/Library/Santana_Zones.pdf
Taylor-Hughlett, J. (2016). Student Self-Assessment—section 3 Learning outcomes, Fall 2016.

19

DANCE EDUCATION

Lynnette Young Overby, Lucy Font and Megan LaMotte

> Every student and child should be able to engage through the power of dance in and out of the classroom to create a positive environment.
>
> *(Emily Ferestein, dance minor capstone, spring 2018)*

Summary

Dance education is a topic of interest to many students, since a studio is a familiar home to them. However, research in this area may be a new experience.

The 2001–2003 Research in Dance Education (RDE) study conducted by the National Dance Education Organization (NDEO) provided invaluable information on the state of completed research in dance education. In this chapter, we provide a brief description of the study followed by the journey of two undergraduate researchers who explored specific topics including interdisciplinary dance education and student engagement.

Introduction

In 2001 the NDEO was the recipient of a three-year grant from the US Department of Education to identify and analyze published and unpublished dance education literature from 1926 – present.

The Research in Dance Education (RDE) project set out to answer the following questions:

- What research exists in dance education? When was it done? Where is it?
- What patterns, trends, and gaps may be identified by analysis of these data?

- What are the implications for understanding the scope of this information for dance, arts education and U.S. education?
- What recommendations for future of dance arts education may grow out of this project?

(Bonbright & Faber, 2004, p. ii)

In a subsequent publication, Bonbright and Faber paint the landscape of dance education research from 1926 to 2002. The historical explanation of dance education is brief, but valuable. Bonbright and Faber discuss dance education's roots in physical education and its shift to the arts in the 1970s. Legislation affecting dance education's inclusion in K–12 education is also touched on, as well as the formation of the NDEO in 1998.

Bonbright and Faber identify subjects of dance education research that they categorize as issues, populations served, and areas of service. They dissect the patterns, trends, and gaps in dance education research and use that as a basis for recommendations for future research in terms of issues, populations served, and areas of service.

The gaps, defined as less than 10% of field attention from 1926 to 2002, provide insight to potential, unsaturated, areas of research. Gaps were found in brain research, world cultures, and interdisciplinary education, among many others. Researchers should focus their efforts to bridge the gaps. The work provides researchers with an opportunity to reflect on how dance education research patterns, trends, and gaps have changed over the years. The publication provides substantive information for future research that will move the field of dance education forward. Included are many topics that could be of interest to undergraduate researchers.

This chapter will focus on the impact of dance education research and scholarship on the educational outcomes of two former University of Delaware undergraduate students, Megan LaMotte and Lucy Font, who were ArtsBridge scholars and conducted research over several years that became a publication in the *Journal of Dance Education* (LaMotte, 2018) and a senior thesis (Font, 2016). Examples of their journey as scholars are included in this chapter. The chapter will also provide dance education topics for future exploration.

Megan's journey

The following reflection by Megan LaMotte provides insight into her journey as a psychology major and dance minor. She describes opportunities to conduct research, and share her findings at conferences, and through publications.

I am so grateful for the opportunity I was given in college to fulfill the role of an ArtsBridge Scholar. Looking back, I realize the breadth of what I learned over those few years. I was a dance minor and psychology major and the ArtsBridge scholar program took my education in both of those fields to the next level. ArtsBridge helped me take the research methods I learned in my psychology classes and marry them with my passion for dance, and introduced me to the scholarship of arts integration. I think what makes the ArtsBridge scholars program so exceptional is that it took my college experience to the next level in many ways. I went from presenting in classrooms, to presenting at national conferences. As a psychology major, I got to be a research assistant and spent many hours entering data. Yet, as an ArtsBridge scholar, I developed my own research study and was in charge of every step from conception to analysis and publication. These experiences are invaluable to me. They are what have shaped my career path as a research professional.

(Megan LaMotte, personal communication)

Abstract: The integrated approach vs. the traditional approach: Analyzing the benefits of a dance and transportation integrated curriculum

The purpose of the study was to examine the effects of a dance and transportation integrated curriculum on student learning and engagement. The curriculum entitled *Consequences of our Actions: Dance and Transportation* synthesized transportation content with the art form of dance. The experimental and control groups were comprised of fifth grade students at a Maryland elementary school. In the spring of 2014, the experimental study was implemented and data was collected in the form of pretests, posttests, and student journals. Analysis of the quantitative data found that the experimental group tested significantly better from the transportation pretests to posttests. The experimental group also tested significantly better than the control group when looking at their transportation posttests. The journals collected displayed high levels of student engagement. What this study suggests is that the instruction of the dance and transportation integrated curriculum facilitated higher levels of student learning and engagement.

Lucy's engagement

Lucy Font, another undergraduate student, focused on the topic of student engagement and dance education for her senior thesis. The following summary of current research includes her findings regarding dance and student engagement accompanied by her reflection.

Dance as form of engagement in the classroom

The concept of student engagement has been studied for decades, and is most often linked to improving student achievement (Fredricks, Blumenfeld, & Paris, 2004). However, more recent approaches identify student engagement as a multidimensional construct (Fredricks, Blumenfeld, & Paris, 2004). Defined as the observable embodiment of motivation, a student's engagement is a strong predictor of his or her academic success in school (O'Donnell, Reeve, & Smith, 2012, p. 334). In order for a student to be engaged with material, he or she must demonstrate active involvement with the learning activity and a commitment to the task at hand (Fredricks, Blumenfeld, & Paris, 2004, p. 60). Fredricks, Blumenfeld, and Paris (2004) therefore suggest that engagement is a multi-faceted construct that exists across three domains: behavior, emotion, and cognition.

Arts integration, and dance integration in particular, allows students to overcome many of the barriers separating them from engaged learning. An arts integration project called Arts for Academic Achievement was implemented across 45 Minneapolis elementary schools in 2003 (Ingram & Seashore, 2003, p. 2). The results of the program were positive for both students and teachers. Researchers reported that the program allowed teachers to better meet the needs of diverse student population. Furthermore, the program "positively impacted the achievement gap" by improving learning in reading and math (Ingram & Seashore, 2003, p. 10).

Additionally, a 2001 study analyzed the effects of a three-year dance integration project implemented in a Minnesota elementary school (Werner). Six classroom teachers and three dance professionals created and taught a dance-integrated math curriculum in a collaborative effort to stimulate students' kinesthetic intelligences while encouraging them to make complex connections. Results showed a significant difference in student attitudes toward math between the experimental group and the control group. In the spring, those students exposed to a dance-integrated curriculum had a more positive attitude toward and enjoyment of mathematics, as indicated by a significantly higher score on the survey (Werner, 2001, p. 3). In general, students in the non-dance class maintained or decreased their survey scores from the fall to the spring (Werner, 2001, p. 5).

In a mixed-methods study on dance integration, Ryan (2014) found that dance-integrated math instruction yielded positive attitudes toward math and dance. In this study, students from two classrooms in Newark, DE, were sampled. Twenty-two students received instruction in a dance-integrated math curriculum, and 16 students were part of a control group that received only math instruction (Ryan, 2014, p. 29). Analysis of both quantitative and qualitative data revealed that the experimental group had increased knowledge of both dance and math concepts (Ryan, 2014, p. 49). Additionally, these students showed positive attitudes toward performance, dance, and math (Ryan, 2014, p. 50). Thus, students exposed to a dance-integrated math curriculum learned more about both the academic content area and the art form, while having a positive experience (Ryan, 2014, p. 52).

A mixed-methods study of dance, math, and student engagement indicated that dance integration engages students in all three domains: behavior, cognition, and emotion (Boccardi, 2015). Seventeen students from a second grade classroom in Newark, DE, were exposed to a dance-integrated math curriculum over the course of three weeks. Math concepts taught included money and time (Boccardi, 2015, p. 20). Data was collected in the form of a quantitative post-survey, along with videotapes, student-created journal entries, and case studies (Boccardi, 2015, p. 25). Results indicated that a dance-integrated math curriculum was behaviorally, emotionally, and cognitively engaging for students, and also provided a positive learning experience (Boccardi, 2015, p. 95).

Lastly, a 2016 study on dance integration and student engagement indicated that dance integration is engaging for students from low-income homes (Font, 2016). Learners within an urban setting were instructed using a researcher-designed dance integrated math curriculum in a summer camp. All 13 participants were from low-income homes in Wilmington, DE. These lessons integrated math concepts and dance concepts. Qualitative data was collected in the form of video recordings and journals, and this data was compared to results from quantitative data, collected in the form of pre- and post-assessments and surveys. Students reported feeling emotionally engaged with the material and showed achievement by improving test scores between the pre- and post-assessments. The findings indicated that dance integration was emotionally, cognitively, and behaviorally engaging for students from low-income homes (Font, 2016, p. 67).

Lucy's reflection

Through the ArtsBridge program, I broadened my knowledge of arts integration as a teaching approach and had the invaluable experience of conducting undergraduate research. I learned how to write an effective research question, about data collection and analysis, and how to present research. I attended several academic conferences as a Scholar, including one international dance and the Child international conference in Copenhagen, Denmark. These opportunities would never have been afforded to me without the ArtsBridge Program. My culminating accomplishment as an ArtsBridge Scholar was the completion of my Honors thesis, titled Adding Movement to Subtract Monotony: The Effects of a Dance-Integrated Mathematics Curriculum on the Engagement of Students from Low-Income Homes. In this thesis, I presented and analyzed the data I'd collected at the Salvation Army summer camp. I further honed the academic writing skills I'd learned as a Scholar to complete a literature review and describe my research methods. My findings were that a dance-integrated mathematics curriculum was cognitively, emotionally, and behaviorally engaging for students from low-income homes. After receiving a BS in Elementary Education, I went on to teach English in Madrid, where I regularly utilize the knowledge and skills I gained as an ArtsBridge Scholar. My research experience as an ArtsBridge Scholar shaped my undergraduate experience and has ultimately made me a better educator. With the guidance of my faculty mentor, I learned how to develop and investigate a research topic and discuss it in an academic paper. The research I conducted as an undergraduate has inspired me to consider the role of dance in the classroom and ultimately made me a more dynamic and effective teacher.

Adding movement to subtract monotony: The effects of a dance-integrated mathematics curriculum on the engagement of students from low-income homes

Lucy Font, senior thesis, University of Delaware, 2016

The objective of this investigation was to determine whether a dance-integrated mathematics curriculum stimulates cognitive, emotional, and behavioral engagement among low-income students in the state of Delaware. Learners within an urban setting were instructed using a researcher-designed dance integrated math curriculum for second-grade students in a summer camp in the state of Delaware. Lessons integrated math concepts (operations and algebraic thinking, numbers and operations in the base ten system, and geometry) and dance concepts (locomotor and non-locomotor movements, levels, shapes, and space). Participants included 13 children, ages 6 to 11, from low-income homes. A concurrent triangulation method was utilized to guide data collection for this mixed methods study. Qualitative data included video recordings and journals. This data was compared with the outcomes of quantitative measures including pre- and post-assessments, pre- and post-surveys, and rubric evaluations of permanent products created by students. Findings from data analyses indicate that a dance-integrated mathematics curriculum was emotionally, cognitively, and behaviorally engaging. These findings suggest that educators can use arts integration to engage their students.

Possible research topics

1. Strategies to keeping students motivated.
2. Inclusion of children with special needs in the classroom.
3. Engaging and promoting learning for students from marginalized backgrounds.
4. Dance as a form of multiculturalism through social justice teaching.
5. Explore how dance and creative movement can be used in classrooms with English language learners.
6. Study the issue of accessibility of dance for low-income students.
7. Research the link between engagement and achievement in the classroom, especially for marginalized students and/or students with special needs.
8. Conduct a cross-sectional study of dance in diverse environments focusing on positive health outcomes.
9. Review current research on the brain and interdisciplinary learning.
10. Conduct case studies on ethnic groups native dance style.
11. Research dance education opportunities and their impact on seniors and the elderly.
12. Research access to dance in after-school and outreach programs for different populations.

Conclusion

The 2001–2003 RDE study conducted by the NDEO provided invaluable information on the state of completed research in dance education. Two undergraduate researchers explored specific topics including interdisciplinary dance and student engagement. Many more dance education topics are ready for exploration by future undergraduate students.

Questions for discussion

1. What questions might future dance education researchers have?
2. What are the gaps in research identified by the NDEO dance study?
3. Why is research on student engagement relevant and necessary? What is the difference between engagement and achievement?
4. What is the intrinsic value and instrumental value of dance education research?
5. What are five examples of environments where dance education research can be conducted?

References

Boccardi, A. (2015). Math is music to our ears: The effects of a music and movement integrated mathematics curriculum on second grade students' engagement with learning. (Unpublished manuscript).

Bonbright, J., & Faber, R. (2004). *Research priorities for dance education: A report to the nation.* Retrieved June 19, 2018 from https://www.ndeo.org/

Font, L. (2016). Adding movement to subtract monotony: The effects of a dance-integrated mathematics curriculum on the engagement of students from low-income homes. (Unpublished manuscript).

Fredricks, J., Blumenfeld, P., & Paris, A. (2004). School engagement: Potential of the concept, state of the evidence. *Review of Educational Research*, 74(1), 59–109.

Ingram, D., & Seashore, K. (2003). *Arts for academic achievement: Summative evaluation report.* Minneapolis, MN: Center for Applied Research and Educational Improvement, College of Education and Hum Dev., University of Minnesota.

LaMotte, M. (2018). The integrated approach versus the traditional approach: Analyzing the benefits of a dance and transportation integrated curriculum. *Journal of Dance Education*, 18 (1), 23–32. https://doi.org/10.1080/15290824.2017.1336667

O'Donnell, A., Reeve, J., & Smith, J. (2012). *Educational psychology*. Hoboken, NJ: Wiley.

Ryan, J. (2014). Math that moves you: A study of the effect of a dance integrated mathematics curriculum supplement on the knowledge and attitudes of second grade students. (Unpublished manuscript).

Werner, L. (2001). Changing student attitudes toward math: Using dance to teach math. Minneapolis, MN: The Center for Applied Research and Educational Improvement, University of Minnesota.

20

ONLINE RESOURCES

April Singleton and Lynnette Young Overby

Summary

This chapter on online resources includes an annotated collection of salient websites and PDFs with a short description about each to help students judge their credibility and learn how to use them. Included are undergraduate research organizations, dance organizations, research tools, current events, and resources related to the various topics included in this text.

Organizations for undergraduate research

British Conference of Undergraduate Research (BCUR)

BCUR, an organization promoting undergraduate research across all disciplines, meets every spring in a different British university where undergraduates submit papers, posters, workshops, and performances to the conference. Abstract submissions, including those from outside of the United Kingdom, are peer-reviewed, and if accepted, are invited to present at the conference. http://www.bcur.org/

Council on Undergraduate Research (CUR)

CUR aims to provide research opportunities to faculty and students at all institutions serving undergraduate students as well as guidance towards successful undergraduate research programs through its publications and activities. The organization also shares the importance of undergraduate research with government institutions such as the US Congress and private foundations. Its resource page provides links to research and presentation opportunities, undergraduate research journals, CUR-sponsored student events, and more for undergraduate students who are conducting faculty-mentored research. https://www.cur.org/

National Collegiate Honors Council (NCHC)

Founded in 1966, NCHC is an educational organization designed to support and promote undergraduate honors education by providing its members with resources, scholarships, training opportunities, and collaborative and exclusive events to build and sustain honors programs and their curriculum. https://www.nchchonors.org/

National Conference of Undergraduate Research (NCUR)

This organization is dedicated to promoting undergraduate research, scholarship, and creativity in all fields of study through its annual conferences for student presentations. Since 1987, NCUR has also been archiving abstracts from the thousands of students who present each year into a searchable database. https://ncurdb. cur.org/ncur2016/archive/Search_NCUR.aspx

Organizations for dance

American Dance Therapy Association (ADTA)

ADTA, the only US organization dedicated to the profession of dance/movement therapy (DMT), is a national and international advocate for the development and expansion of the field. It aims to stimulate communication among dance/movement therapists through social media, an academic journal, and an original newsletter, as well as holding an annual conference and sponsoring webinars for continuing education, networking, and the advancement of scholarship in DMT. https://adta.org/

Dancers Alliance (DA)

DA works to be the unified voice of a nationwide community of dancers. The organization improves the careers of professional dancers and choreographers by negotiating equitable rates and working conditions for non-union workers as well as representing them on union boards and committees. https://www.dancersalliance.org/

Dance and the Child International (daCi)

daCi is an internationally dedicated non-profit organization that promotes the growth and development of dance for children around the world. By fostering the exchange and collaboration of all forms of dance through a triennial conference, projects, and funding, it aims to promote the belief that every young person, regardless of their ethnic, gender, and cultural identity, should have equal access and opportunity to dance. https://www.daci.international/en/

Dance Studies Association (DSA)

DSA, an international organization of dance scholars, educators, and artists, has a resource page that links users to open calls (opportunities to present research, apply for fellowships, and present work), job opportunities, working groups, and external resources. https://dancestudiesassociation.org/resources

Dance/USA

Dance/USA represents the interests of the national dance community by advocating for the development of national arts policies that recognize and strengthen the community before federal government agencies such as the White House. Its Advocacy and Visibility page shares information on key issues, outside resources, congressional visits, and more. https://www.danceusa.org/advocacy

International Association for Dance Medicine & Science (IADMS)

IADMS is an international network between dance and medicine where dance medicine practitioners, dance educators, dance scientists, and dancers share a goal of enhancing health, well-being, training, and performance in dance by cultivating medical, scientific, and educational excellence. https://www.iadms.org/

International Choreographers' Organization and Networking Services (Dance ICONS)

Dance ICONS, a global network for choreographers of all experience levels, nationalities, and genres, offers a cloud-based platform for knowledge exchange, collaboration, inspiration, and debate for creators all over the world. Its resources page offers links to a wide variety of choreography competitions, funding opportunities, dance organizations and more for their users. http://162.144.59.103/index.php

National Dance Education Organization (NDEO)

NDEO is an organization that provides professional development, networking forums, honor societies, journals, research and advocacy tools for teachers, administrators, and students in the field of dance arts education. http://www.ndeo.org

Research resources

Dance: Interdisciplinary research

Introduces the KSL Summon Search Engine and the EBSCO database that are equipped with finding-related subjects across different disciplines. Summon, a Google-like search engine, uses a relevancy algorithm to search across both online and print resources for information, whereas EBSCO is a multidisciplinary database that collects resources from many areas of study, including dance. https://researchguides.case.edu/c.php?g=172308&p=1136555

Dance movement notation

This is a collection of online resources for students who are interested in including notation as a research tool:

- https://labaninstitute.org/what-we-do/research-development/
- https://labaninstitute.org/what-we-do/research-development/bibliography/
- http://www.dancenotation.org/
- http://ickl.org/resources/resources/
- http://www.mars.dti.ne.jp/~monako/laban/index.html
- https://www.lodc.org/
- http://isis.cnd.fr/notateurs/spip.php?article48
- http://imsmovement.com/index.html
- https://www.labanguild.org.uk/magazine/magazine-index/
- http://movescapecenter.com/shop/
- http://ead.ohiolink.edu/xtf-ead/view?docId=ead/xOU-TR0002.xml;query=
- https://roehamptondance.com/dance-archives-at-roehampton/a nn-hutchinson-guest-collection/
- http://www.adli.us/

Google Scholar

Google Scholar, working similarly to its parent search engine, provides a simple way to search for academic resources. From one place, users can search across many disciplines and types of sources, including articles, books, online repositories and more. https://scholar.google.com/

The Purdue Online Writing Lab: Research and citation resources— Research resources

This page offers users a variety of information on how to conduct and use research properly, as well as formatting guides using APA, MLA, Chicago, and AMA citation styles. https://owl.english.purdue.edu/owl/section/2/

Sample video projects

This list is a compilation of links to videos that showcase projects incorporating the research of a certain topic with dance:

- Katherine Williams, In the Field, A Showcase of Undergraduate Research at Illinois, https://www.youtube.com/watch?v=8LxvpCFU0pA
- Dance it out with responsive LED costumes, https://www.youtube.com/wa tch?v=C2MlEbGrLz4

- How Dance, Statistics and Research relate for a Loyola Undergraduate Student, https://www.youtube.com/watch?v=Xin5HY2TrHw
- Cuban Dance Research Project, https://www.youtube.com/watch?v=KPKfGBCJYlU
- Prof. Robin Kish, Dance, Chapman University, https://www.youtube.com/watch?v=QDhd8oHRl90
- Dance student incorporates GoPro cameras in her senior thesis, https://www.youtube.com/watch?v=umQmHn24yLU

TED Talks—Research resources

Known for its inspirational videos, a search for dance topics yields a variety of results such as breaking gender roles, overcoming cancer, and using bionic limbs with dance, as well as many other interesting videos. https://www.ted.com/talks?topics%5B%5D=dance

University of South Carolina Office of Research—Tips & tools

This page links users to navigation tools that aim to guide undergraduate researchers through their rights, responsibilities, and resources. Through the site, users can learn how to get credit for their research, make quality presentations, publish their work, and much more. http://www.sc.edu/our/tips.shtml

Current events in dance

What difference does dance make? Critical conversations across dance, physical activity, and public health

With contributions from the director of an established community-based dance organization, a local authority public health commissioner, and three academic researchers (a sociologist, cultural geographer, and technologist), this research fosters a critical conversation about how dance exists within current discussions about physical activity, public health, and sports policy. Through their dynamic dialogue, they gain an understanding of how evaluating dance as physical activity will require people to work against currently constrained conversation and insight on how exploring the discursive tension can be substantial towards the creation of policies. https://www.tandfonline.com/doi/pdf/10.1080/19406940.2016.1238404?needAccess=true

ArtsJournal—Dance

This page offers links to dance articles that have been compiled from blogs, newspapers, magazines, and publications from around the world that feature current events in the arts and culture of today. The list holds topics ranging from the unionization of freelance dancers, the establishment of a Trans-led dance company, a ballet teacher who teaches dance to children in wheelchairs, and more. http://www.artsjournal.com/category/dance

Resources connected to specific topics

Dance therapy

Dance/movement therapy and integrative medicine

In this video sponsored by the American Dance Therapy Association, Dr. Sherry W. Goodill gives a short talk on the benefits of dance/movement therapy (DMT) as a complementary and integrative health practice. Starting with a description of a bidirectional relationship between mind and body, she continues to move through the history of DMT as the knowledge of the practice is expanded. https://www.youtube.com/watch?v=uz6S9LQvvHQ&t=105s&index=4&list=PLrbXrO8yG6hpvRWRnNTij7_CWTt2Th2J

Effect of dance/motor therapy on the cognitive development of children

This paper describes in detail what the theory of dance motor therapy is and the impact it can have on the cognitive development of children due to its exercise of intelligence, spirituality, discovery, and spontaneity with the creation of the art, as well as the physical sensitivity and awareness a person gains from dancing.   http://www.openaccesslibrary.org/images/XEW191_Asmita_Vilas_Balgaonkar.pdf

Good Therapy—Dance/movement therapy

Good Therapy, an organization that offers access to therapists, treatment centers, and mental health resources, has a page on dance/movement therapy (DMT) that shares a list of issues dance therapy can help with, why the practice is effective, the principles of this type of healing, the differences it has from regular dancing, and the history and philosophy behind DMT.

   https://www.goodtherapy.org/learn-about-therapy/types/dance-movement-therapy

Public scholarship

Imagining America: Artists and scholars in public life

This organization has a mission to create democratic spaces where publicly engaged arts, design, and the humanities thrive. A focus of this organization is on changing policies, structures and practices at colleges and universities that will value the contributions of the engaged scholar. https://www.engagedscholarship.org

Public: A Journal of Imagining America

Public is an arts, humanities and design peer-reviewed multi-media e-journal focused on public scholarship. It shares projects, resources, and new ideas surrounding the arts, as well as how they can connect with other disciplines. http://public.imaginingamerica.org

Campus Compact

Campus Compact is a national organization that supports student and faculty engagement with the community. Its resources page has an extensive list of blog posts, books, publications, civic action plans, external websites, press releases and more to help inform its users about public scholarship. https://www.compact.org

International Association for Research on Service Learning and Community Engagement (IARSLCE)

This organization facilitates dialogue and information exchange about service learning research for students, funders, faculty, and community partners. Its *International Journal of Research on Service-Learning and Community Engagement* is a peer-reviewed online journal that discusses the latest research in the area. http://www.researchslce.org

Choreography

Choreographic process

The following links are a culmination of articles on the choreographic process and how to make a successful piece through the potential hardships:

- https://www.nyfa.edu/student-resources/how-to-choreograph-a-dance-when-you-are-stuck/
- https://www.contemporary-dance.org/choreography.html
- https://socialdance.stanford.edu/Syllabi/Choreography.htm
- http://dancemagazine.com.au/2017/01/5-ways-to-look-at-creativity-to-enhance-your-choreography-and-your-life/

Performance Research—On choreography

In this issue of the *Performance Research* journal, the notion of choreography is explored as it has changed throughout history, from simple dance composition towards an art that uses a wider range of conceptual tools, materials, and strategies. To emphasize this shift, over 20 articles have been gathered to share different aspects of choreography, including perspectives that consider the choreography of the pedestrian, practical research and dance historiography, and political statements against the exploitation of textile workers.

http://www.performance-research.org/past-issue-detail.php?issue_id=43

Dance and culture

Dance ethnology and the anthropology of dance

This article by Adrienne L. Kaeppler from the *Dance Research Journal* focuses on dance studies by anthropologists, ethnologists, and other Indigenous scholars and how their work with dance is presented. Their interpretations of dance's impact on societal, cultural, and political movements are also emphasized in the article. http://www.jstor.org/stable/1478285

National Archive of Data on Arts and Culture (NADAC)

NADAC is an online repository that covers a wide variety of topics in arts and culture and has a search navigation that is useful for users looking for specific pieces of information. With over 278 datasets, 500 publications, and 76,875 variables to pull from, this archive provides a plethora of useful data.

https://www.icpsr.umich.edu/icpsrweb/NADAC/search/studies

Sharing culture through dance

This is a compilation of websites, articles, and videos that exemplify how people can express their culture through the movement of the body and performance a dance piece:

- https://www.arhu.umd.edu/news/understanding-culture-through-its-dance-traditions
- https://vimeo.com/32808763
- https://www.tandfonline.com/doi/pdf/10.1080/07303084.2000.10605161
- https://www.citizen-times.com/story/news/local/2017/02/02/black-history-culture-told-through-dance/97103982/

Teaching the anthropology of dance

Written by Michelle Hagman, this article shares a lesson plan that can be used to introduce undergraduate students to the anthropology of dance, as well as guiding the students to topics they may want to research. The general website also has a search engine that can be used to find journal articles relating to specific topics in relation to anthropology. https://culanth.org/fieldsights/867-teaching-the-anthropology-of-dance

Dance history

A very brief overview of dance history

This article by Typhani R. Harris, PhD gives short descriptions of five different time periods of dance in history—primitive, ancient, medieval, renaissance, and contemporary.   https://educationcloset.com/wp-content/uploads/2014/08/A-VERY-Brief-Overview-of-Dance-History.pdf

Dance online: Dance in video

With selections covering most genres of dance from ballet, to improvisation, as well as the pioneers of these different forms of dance, this database contains productions and documentaries by the most influential performers and companies of the 20th century. https://search.alexanderstreet.com/daiv

What does dance history have to do with dancing?

In this essay, Elizabeth Kattner, PhD explores the ways of incorporating dance history into the lives of everyday dancers that is relevant and supportive to their careers as students, performers, and choreographers. The work also shows readers how they can study history through movement as well as with more conventional resources such as books, papers, images, and videos. https://www.tandfonline.com/doi/full/10.1080/15290824.2015.1036435?src=recsys&

Dance science

Journal of Dance Medicine & Science (JDMS)

JDMS brings a collection of up-to-date information on topics such as biomechanics, physical therapy, dance education, and many more with original articles focusing on the identification, treatment, rehabilitation, and prevention of illness and injuries in dancers. https://www.iadms.org/page/47

PubMed

PubMed, a free resource maintained by the National Center for Biotechnology Information (NCBI), contains over 28 million citations for biomedical literature from MEDLINE, life science journals, and online books. Through a simple search, the site gives access to citations and abstracts related to the life sciences, behavioral sciences, chemical sciences, and bioengineering as well as access to more relevant websites and links to NCBI resources. https://www.ncbi.nlm.nih.gov/pubmed

Dance psychology/cognition

Performance anxiety

The following is a compilation of articles about overcoming performance anxiety and turning that negative energy into a motivation for dancers:

- http://laurastanyer.blogspot.com/2011/06/stage-fright-performance-anxiety-and.html
- https://www.dancemagazine.com/performance-anxiety-2569045254.html
- http://www.anxietycoach.com/performanceanxiety.html
- https://www.dancespirit.com/making-stick-2326466070.html

Psychology Tomorrow Magazine (PTM)

PTM, with a mission to provide cutting-edge information and technology surrounding psychology, examines the work of academics, philosophers, writers, and artists that may challenge conventional psychologies. This page shows the search results for articles that contain the word "dance," giving users a wide variety of links that explore different aspects of psychology, including examples like recovering from trauma, exploring female sexuality, and impacting emotions through dance. http://psychologytomorrowmagazine.com/tag/dance/

Scientific American—The neuroscience of dance

This article in *Scientific American* by Steven Brown and Lawrence M. Parsons explores concepts of dance as a fundamental form of expression, an artform that requires special mental skills, and a rhythmic version of unconscious entertainment. They also showcase results of recent-brain imaging studies that reveal how the brain performs as people dance. http://www.neuroarts.org/pdf/SciAm_Dance.pdf

Dance technology

Dance Tech

Dance Tech explores the potential of the new internet technologies for knowledge production and distribution on body-based artistic practices and its intersections with other disciplines such as new media, architecture, philosophy, anthropology and more. The platform combines many services including user generated content platforms, collaborative environments, and interdisciplinary production methods for its users. http://www.dance-tech.net/

PAJ: A Journal of Performance and Art

PAJ brings together innovative work in performance art, dance, technology and more, in thoughtful dialogue with critical essays, artists' writings, interviews, plays, drawings, and notations, with extended coverage of performance, festivals, and books. PAJ's online website also carries podcasts, video, and audio clips about advancements in performance art. https://www.jstor.org/journal/pajjperfart

Troika Ranch

This company combines dance, theatre, and new media. Dawn Stoppiello and Mark Coniglio, co-founders and artistic directors is the creator of the award-winning software Isadora®, a flexible graphic programming environment that provides interactive control over digital media. http://troikaranch.org

Dance education

The Dance Education Literature and Research Descriptive Index (DELRdi)

The DELRdi is a searchable index of literature and research that informs users about the implementation and learnings of dance education. The database contains extensive descriptions of several thousand literary works, including theses, dissertations, journal articles, and more, that can be searched by the citation information, content, research method, research characteristics, and keywords. http://www.ndeo.org/content.aspx?page_id=1106&club_id=893257

Dance education matters: Rebuilding postsecondary dance education for twenty-first century relevance and resonance

This article explores four big challenges of dance education in the 21st century: curricular equity, expansive dance education programs, graduate study opportunities, and national leadership. With a push to expand the current curriculum to include teachings of a private studio, commercial-sector, dance in a community and related teaching professions, the author provides recommendations and strategies to develop relevant dance education programs beyond current standards. https://doi.org/10.1080/15290824.2010.529761

Dance in interdisciplinary teaching and learning

This article focuses on the benefits of interdisciplinary dance education where the topics involved have a complementary balance of weight in a standardized curriculum, rather than dance being just an engagement activity for students. Specifically, this article exemplifies a proposed framework by integrating dance and anthropology together into one unique opportunity to learn a new perspective. https://doi.org/10.1080/15290824.2006.10387312

Moving social justice: Challenges, fears, and possibilities in dance education

When it comes to teaching dance, there are certain social justice commitments and preparations that teachers must be aware of, and this article explores those responsibilities from the perspective of two dance educators and formal administrators in higher education. As they research the influences of multiculturalism on dance teacher education, they also explore the limitations of a multicultural movement in the field due to the present misconceptions about different cultures, genders, ethnicities, and socioeconomic backgrounds. http://www.ijea.org/v11n6/v11n6.pdf

Say it through dance

To answer the question, "How can I use my body to express ideas through movement," the author created this guide to help educators teach their students the basics of dance and what they can gain from the art. With built-in lessons, worksheets, activities, and glossaries, this is a good foundation for most types of dance education for grade school children. https://rover.edonline.sk.ca/system/guides/big_ideas_7_dance.pdf

Journal of Dance Education (JODE)

This publication presents the latest developments in dance education research by sharing scholarly and practical articles that are relevant to many different segments of the dance community. To help dance educators around the world stay current in the classroom, this journal explores topics like dance training, curriculum, teaching methodology, assessments, collaboration, dance advocacy and more through the four issues released to subscribers every year. https://www.ndeo.org/jode

Dance philosophy

Dance as a way of knowing

This article explores dance as movement through space; an art form that encourages being physically present in the world and may be considered as a way of knowing. Linking to a podcast discussing this topic, the philosophical conversation aims to answer questions about what audiences can learn from watching dancers, and what lessons there are to learn about human perception and action. https://www.philosophytalk.org/blog/dance-way-knowing

Philosophy and dance—Dancing is thinking

This article provides a perspective on dance philosophy that merges mind and body into one dynamic form where physical and mental movements complement each other through dance. With the concept of moving thoughts, more philosophers today are starting to see dancing as a form of thinking itself, where the process of thought is expressed through the process of movement. https://www.goethe.de/en/kul/tut/gen/tan/20509666.html

The philosophy of dance

As a performance art, one of many aspects of dance is the entertaining of a crowd and the appreciation audience members may gain from watching dancers on a stage. With the focus on performing for others, this article explores the philosophy of dance that has developed as a subset of philosophical aesthetics, considering philosophical questions such as what the nature of dance is and how dance performances are appreciated, experienced and perceived. https://plato.stanford.edu/entries/dance/

INDEX

Registered Dance/Movement Therapist
(R-DMT) 85
reliability of researcher 44
research design 22, 45
Research in Dance Education (RDE) 158
research journal, keeping of 11
research methods *see* methods
results of research 47
rhetorical situation 72–3, rhetorical triangle
32–3, *see also* Aristotle
ritual 118
Roberts, R. 56
Rostas, S. 119
Ryan, J. 161

Same Story, Different Countries (SSDC) 57, 96
Sandel, S. 86
Santana & Iazetta 153
Schoene, L. M. 135
scholarly community 68
scholarly process 40
search terms 10
secondary sources 10, 38
Sevdalis & Keller 143
Sketches—The Life of Harriet E. Wilson in Dance, Poetry and Music 95–6
Skloot, R. 27
Snowber, C. 55
somatic education 133; research topics 135–6
standard deviation 51
statistical analysis 36–7
statistical terms 51
structural analysis 36, 52
subsections of journal articles 42–3
surveys 36–7, 49
Sweigard, L. 133
symposium of student research 73–5

Taylor & Estanol 142
Taylor & Taylor 142
Taylor-Hughlett, J. 153
themes in research data 15
theoretical approach 40–1, 46
timeline for research 22–3
topic areas in dance 21, refining of 18–20
triangulation of data 33–4
truncation symbols 10
Turabian style 13, 65–6

undergraduate research terminology xiii, 1,
see also URSCA
unemployment and underemployment of
college graduates 70
univariate analysis 49
URSCA (undergraduate research,
scholarship, and creative activity) xiii, 2
US National Library of Medicine 134

Vannette, D. 35
variables 43–4
vulnerable populations 29

Warburton, E. C. 143
Warburton, et al. 143
Werner, L. 161
Wilmerding & Krasnow 133
Wilson & Moffett 56, 57
Winters, A. F. 86
Witkin, H. 144
Women of Consequence—Ambitious, Ancillary and Anonymous 96
World Health Organization 28
written communication skills 71–72

Zech, et al. 134

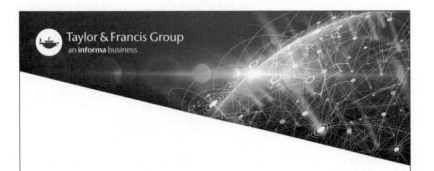